Praise for *Never Alone*

"Have you ever had your heart broken? Have you ever felt abandoned, unloved? If you have, you will find a friend in these pages. With disarming transparency, Tiffany walks us through her own heartbreak to the glorious realization of this truth: she has never been alone, and neither have we."
—*Sheila Walsh*, author of *In the Middle of the Mess*

"In her powerful book, *Never Alone*, Tiffany reaches down a hand of been-there hope to those who still wonder if anyone sees their aching loneliness—to the ones who live with a perpetual sense of being on the outside, of looking in through an impenetrable barrier at an unreachable place of true belonging.

The richest theology combines study with story, especially one's own personal story of pain, grace, and redemption. With raw honesty, beautiful imagery, Tiffany brings flesh-and-blood life to this biblical truth: Jesus. Is. With. Us. Always. This book is for those (like me and everyone I know) who need this reminder and a fresh look at how the 'with-ness' of Jesus changes everything, even in our most desolate seasons."
—*Jodi Detrick*, author of *The Jesus-Hearted Woman*

"Tiffany so beautifully articulates stories of rejection, with which we can all identify, only to make way for acceptance in the presence of Jesus. What a beautiful extension of Tiffany's heart, so that we too can call out our pain in order to usher in wholeness and freedom. *Never Alone* is a must-read!"
—*Kelsey Chapman*, Radiant Podcast

"One of the most profound women of spiritual influence and insight for encouraging us in our walk with our Abba Father!"
—*Josh Dunn*, president and publisher, Premier Media

"Tiffany's story, shared with vulnerability and remarkable insight, invites us into meaningful reflection on our own lives and the truth of God's Word. This is a must-read for anyone who needs a reminder that they are *Never Alone!*"
—*Harmony Dust*, MSW, founder and executive director
of Treasures Ministries

"*Never Alone* is a boldly intimate portrait of the journey to healing and wholeness. Tiffany's vulnerability, tenderness, and wisdom unveil page by page the heart of God toward those who are brokenhearted. This book is a must-read that will give you the courage to face your pain and embrace the unfailing love of Jesus!"

—**Nicole Reyes**, writer, speaker, and director
of Liberty Foundation, NYC

"We were not designed to make decisions and live our lives alone; still, loneliness and isolation plague our generation. With her powerful storytelling and relatable content, Tiffany feels like a friend. She is relentless in her encouragement, in her passion for freedom, and in her desire to communicate the love of Jesus to us. She lives what she preaches and writes, which gives her a unique authority to speak truth. I believe God has created her to bring transformation, love, and compassion everywhere she goes. Her book will not only bring freedom but also provide a safe place for women to share, grow, and change."

—**Ashley Abercrombie**, director of Liberty City, NYC

"Up close, Tiffany is a spark, a fire, something different. Her own story is one I hope more people will hear. Her writing is rich and fiery and full of voice. Read it slowly. Don't gulp the words down; instead, sip and savor them, and rest in the warmth of the revelation that you are *Never Alone*."

—**Brian Dolleman**, author of *Peace & Rest* and
pastor of NWLife Church

"Through courageous honesty, Tiffany Bluhm presents a map and compass to the one longing to find the seemingly elusive reality of God's ever-present love. For those struggling to navigate the deep and troubled waters of the soul, *Never Alone* is a gift to your life."

—**David Resinger**, senior pastor, Redeem Church

Exchanging
Your Tender Hurts
for God's Healing
Grace

never alone

Tiffany
Bluhm

ABINGDON PRESS
NASHVILLE

NEVER ALONE
EXCHANGING YOUR TENDER HURTS FOR GOD'S HEALING GRACE

Copyright © 2018 by Abingdon Press

Library of Congress Cataloging-in-Publication Data has been requested.

ISBN 978-1-5018-4863-6

18 19 20 21 22 23 24 25 26 27—10 9 8 7 6 5 4 3 2 1

MANUFACTURED IN THE UNITED STATES OF AMERICA

For Derek, Jericho, and Kingston
Home is wherever I'm with you.

Contents

Introduction

*I*n my early twenties, before a husband and kids came on the scene, I was a morning person. Up early, tea in hand, sitting in a cushy chair by the window as I poured out my thoughts into a trusty journal. By 9:00 p.m. I was snug in my sweatpants, hair in a bun, and dozing off to sleep. One night, in particular, I was cuddled in bed around 8:30 p.m. and heard the faint sound of footsteps making their way up the carpeted stairs of my townhouse. My roommate had texted that she'd be out for the night, unsure of what time she would return. From my bed, I called out her name a few times to see if it was her. I didn't hear an answer. I froze. Too terrified to even reach for my phone to call for help, I sunk deep in the covers. The only sound I heard was my own heart beating out of my chest. In a pool of sweat, I whispered my roommate's name once more, as if anyone could hear me from inside my bedroom. Again, I heard no answer.

Growing up, my worst nightmare was the idea of being attacked while sleeping in bed. Maybe it was too many scary movies or my own imagination hard at work. But each night as a child, it took me a considerable amount of time to fall asleep because I was mortified I would be attacked lying alone in my room.

So there I was, with two decades' worth of bad dreams tucked in my sheets, paralyzed by the monsters in my own mind. Within two minutes I had all but jumped into my own grave. With someone outside my bedroom door, I knew this was the end. Here I was, alone, with an intruder in my house. With no defense, I felt totally helpless. I had no one to scare off the boogieman. No one to protect me from the unknown. I felt completely hopeless in saving myself. I had no stock in my ability to fight off my attacker.

After nearly fifteen minutes, I decided I could not just sit there. At the very least, I needed to switch on the light. With fear dripping from every pore of my body, I mustered enough guts to address the intruder head on. I swung the door open and slapped the light switch on ready to shout as loud as I possibly could. To my surprise I found my room-mate puttering around the house. She looked at me with a smile and said, "Hi, how's your night?"

To which I replied with a straight face, "Well, I thought I was going to die an early death. I called out your name about fifteen minutes ago and didn't hear a reply. So, I assumed the absolute worst and anticipated I was about to die alone from a phantom intruder!"

As my dread turned to lighthearted laughter, I couldn't believe the array of emotions I felt in a mere matter of minutes. Of all things that terrified me the most, being alone was the worst. When we're alone, every isolating thought holds us captive. We feel helpless, hopeless, and forgotten.

As little girls, we feared playing alone on the playground. In middle school, we feared sitting alone at lunch. In high school, we feared going alone to the prom. As adults, we fear we may never marry or have children. We fear our husbands may leave us. We fear we will be left to our solitary selves to fight the hardest battles of our lives. We spend our lives doing our absolute best to prove we are lovable and valuable, never to be ignored or left alone.

While season after season brings fresh mercy and unforeseen misery, the good Lord is available to each of us. The same Lord who sat with harlots, beggars, and the blind sits with you and me. He's patient and kind. Strong and brave. We may test His limits, doubt

His faithfulness, or walk away, but He is always good to us. No matter what.

I am not alone. You are not alone.

The words of this book are an offering to you. An offering in hopes to encourage your heart no matter what season of life you are in. They share about the God who not only gave us life but also gave us His Son as our first companion. The One for whom our soul longs. I have discovered without a doubt that life is hard but Christ is sovereign. He is near. Whether in times of tears or bouts of laughter, He is near. Whether in singing or silence, He is near.

We will find that as our plans, hearts, and lives change, He does not miss a beat. What we may have mistook for His absence was only our mind questioning His goodness and grace. We will never escape His love. We do not possess that kind of power. If we are willing, we will discover the sacred truth that we, indeed, are never alone.

As you thumb through these pages, I pray you receive a fresh revelation of God's mercy. Like a windy day, with gusts that remind you that the unforeseen is powerful and all-encompassing, would you delight in His compassion for you, His patience and mercy, His love and grace?

CHAPTER ONE

Shame

*W*ith middle school girls squished on both sides of me, I sat between them as their "fearless" youth group leader on a cushy church pew. These bright-eyed girls were full of faith as they threw their prayers to God, believing He would answer. After hands rose in worship and heads bowed in prayer, we feverishly took notes from the guest preacher. The preacher man, with his youth pastor–like faux hawk and distressed jeans, fervidly shared the gospel message with the young- sters, as many of us were on the edge of our seats. At the close of his sermon, he held up a kabuki mask explaining how God beckons us to remove our masks, exposing our raw hearts. I smirked at his cheesy, predictable youth-group analogy.

He went on for some time, sticking proudly to his example of the kabuki mask. As he wrapped up his sermon he instructed the crowd to bow their heads and pray. He asked each of us to remove his or her "masks" and to be honest with God. To fall in line and set the exam- ple for the sweet youth-group girls sitting around me, I repeated the prayer under my breath, asking God to remove any mask I might have been wearing, to get to my heart, to walk in the light and fullness of all He had for me. Next thing I knew, I found myself hunched over in the pew scratching at my face. This prayer begun in genuine honesty changed to one of earnest desperation. I was blown to bits by what I felt. Pain. A dull pain. In the depth of my belly, I felt alone and in the dark. I felt like a deserted little girl. I was unable to explain why I felt so bleak. So achy.

There I was, the barely-out-of-high-school youth leader, scratching at my face like a toddler. I groped around the ground for anything to comfort me, anything to save me. Hot tears poured from my eyes; I was overcome with the murky emotions that bubbled to the surface of my heart. Only later, in counseling, did my therapist explain that when a baby fails to cope she is driven to rage, hitting and scratching herself. I was aware, yet again, that I had unresolved issues that I could not button up.

The feelings I later identified as loneliness, abandonment, and rejection that erupted during the youth service first made me their slave when I was four years old. Tiny tears dripped into my pink plastic sippy cup as I wondered why on earth my mama did not want me. Thoughts twisted in my head: *What did I do that was so bad? What if I apologize? Is it because I am a girl? Does she ever think about me?* At four years old, I was aware that my dark skin did not match the skin of my parents or brothers. Their skins boasted a creamy whiteness while mine looked like muddy water.

Only by the love of Jesus do we exchange
our shackles of shame for the robe
of freedom.

Later, at seven years old, I still could not put it all together. Why did everyone have these common stories of a hospital delivery and Olan Mills baby pictures? No trauma at birth. No lost mama never to be met. No daddy never to know of her existence. I was sodden with grief, without words to articulate my heaviness.

I guess that's the affliction of shame on a young soul, a trauma one cannot explain. It's the voice of shame that whispers: "You are different. You are broken. You always will be." You are, simultaneously, not enough and too much. Shame is worn like a corset tied so tight that it makes it hard to breathe. Full of disgust, we look in the mirror, ashamed of ourselves, our stories.

Brené Brown, in her book *Daring Greatly*, writes:

> Shame derives its power from being unspeakable. That's why it loves perfectionists—it's so easy to keep us quiet. If we cultivate enough awareness about shame to name it and speak to it, we've basically cut it off at the knees. Shame hates having words wrapped around it. If we speak shame, it begins to wither. Just the way exposure to light was deadly for the gremlins, language and story bring light to shame and destroy it.
>
> Just like Roosevelt advised, when we dare greatly we will err and we will come up short again and again. There will be failures and mistakes and criticism. If we want to be able to move through the difficult disappointments, the hurt feelings, and the heartbreaks that are inevitable in a fully lived life, we can't equate defeat with being unworthy of love, belonging, and joy. If we do, we'll never show up and try again.[1]

Shame. Once it happens it can never un-happen. It affects how we think, feel, and relate to one another. It gives us a false sense of self, a fragmented view of our soul. We can feel shattered under the weight of loss. The pains of neglect or rejection leave a scar on us. The scars will always be part of our story. They won't be the end of the story, only the beginning. While shame can never un-happen, it can certainly be redeemed. We can show up for our own lives. Lives marked by grace and acceptance, not guilt and shame.

A shamed heart shapes our view of God, His love, His nearness, and His restorative grace. If we dare to trust Him, even though we don't fully understand how He operates in our lives, the distressed pieces of our soul can be resurrected into something beautiful. Something whole. No matter the source of our shame, the wound is dressed the same way. Not through self-help. Not through applause from others. Only by the love of Jesus do we exchange our shackles of shame for the robe of freedom.

The Never-Ending Cycle

I was told she made her way to the orphanage, birthed me, then left. She didn't sign any papers. She left. With no way to track her down. The caregivers at the orphanage waited for a couple months, wondering if she might change her mind, come back, and take me with her. She didn't. Before long I was given the name Abhilasha. I was one of more than twenty-five million orphans in India. Although orphanage caregivers were far outnumbered by a seemingly endless influx of orphans, the caregivers truly believed each orphan's life was not meaningless; there was something for each of us.

Shame never lets us rest. It reminds us how we feel about ourselves when we'd rather forget. It's a mark of something deeper.

I own just one baby picture of myself, taken at five months. I'm wearing a simple cloth diaper with my moppy black hair piled atop my head. My pursed lips appear to be permanently carved on my face. Every time I look at that picture my heart drops. Even at five months old I was scared and unsure of everything around me. Those overwhelming emotions of fear and uncertainty, my demons, were already there for me to fight, not only as a child but also as an adolescent, and later still as an adult.

Shame never lets us rest. It reminds us how we feel about ourselves when we'd rather forget. It's a mark of something deeper. It evokes emotions that cause us to question why we wallow in them day after day. Yet, every shameful thought in us has a story, a birthplace deep in our core. It grows as we grow. Shame threads itself through our ideas, dreams, and hopes. It convinces us we aren't good enough, strong enough, or worthy enough for anyone's love and affection.

Regardless whether our shame stems from abandonment, abuse, neglect, or loss, we believe we are defective, rejected, and just plain broken. The other women in our life may be able to keep it together, parent well-behaved children, sport a size 4, and flirt with their husbands like newlyweds, but not us. Shame keeps us from closing the gap of what we think life should be like to who we really are. Deep down, we aren't OK with who we are, what's happened to us, and where we're headed. The devastating effects of shame can be healed, but not alone. We need a Helper, a Savior, to rewrite our story and renew our thinking. We need Him to tell us we aren't beyond repair. We need to know it won't always be like this, feeling like we can't get ahead, stuck in a forsaken cycle of life.

The Lonely in Families

A small-town family from Washington State went through the three-year process to adopt an orphan from India. They adopted me when I was a year and a half old. I was suddenly part of a family: a father, a mother, and two brothers, six and eight years older than me. My adoptive father was a firefighter and fire extinguisher technician for the military. My adoptive mother was a homemaker. My oldest brother, Teddy, had brain damage. Although he was nearly ten years old when I was adopted, he still had the mentality of a toddler. My other brother, Tim, was cheeky and sweet. He played the big brother to both Teddy and me.

All together we made a family that had both a child with disabilities and an international adoptee. This became my family. We were our own brand of odd. I grew to love my brothers and to give my parents grief, just as all little girls are entitled to do.

The funny thing about adoption is that for the family who is adopting, they often have stars in their eyes about what adoption should look like when adding a newcomer to their home. The truth is, adoption originates in abandonment. Inviting a bedraggled child, who hasn't experienced a healthy home life before, into a home is about as trouble-free as bathing a cat. Rooted in trauma, adoption is only the first step in a long road to healing; and for the adoptee and the family, the road is rocky and rough.

A completed adoption doesn't presume a heart made whole. A new marriage doesn't presume a heart made whole. New friendships don't presume a heart made whole. The broken pieces of our lives will follow us until we surrender them to someone who can fix them. Surrender and healing is a choice. A long road. Healing comes from confronting dark parts of the soul and choosing restoration, incident-by-incident, ache-by-ache, pain-by-pain.

And healing takes time. It doesn't happen instantly with a new surname or a green card. It doesn't happen instantly with new parents or new brothers. It doesn't happen instantly with a new husband or child. It doesn't happen instantly with a new job or applause. It happens at last when a soul surrenders to Jesus, choosing His love and His grace. It happens when peace, forgiveness, and a renewed mind, by the power of the Holy Spirit, work inside an ashamed ragamuffin. It happens when insight from those who have walked the road before, build up the soul that's been traumatized.

It's not impossible. It's not out of reach. Freedom is ours to claim.

Scorn the Shame

I unwrapped my bologna sandwich from my hot pink lunchbox and did my best to hide my excitement as I snagged a seat next to my potential best friend, a transfer student new to the third grade. Since our school was small, just two classrooms for grades K–6, I was eager to learn everything about the new girl. Before I could even utter a measly "Hello," she hastily gathered her juice box, turkey sandwich, and Fruit Roll-Up to find a new spot at another table. I was baffled. Confounded as to why she would flee in my presence, I pursued her. There were only nine kids in the third grade, slim pickings in the way of new friends. When I finally mustered up the courage to ask her why she left, she answered, "I've never met anyone brown before. I'm scared to be with you. You are so different."

In February, she wouldn't eat the cookies I brought to the Valentine's Day party. I assured her they were delicious, shortbread with red crystal sprinkles, my favorite. She quietly took them off of her plate and put them on a napkin. I had no words for the feelings she left me with that day. I didn't have a clue what to make of it. But I could feel the heat of disgrace on my face.

Back then, I wouldn't have been able to explain it like I can now. I know the word for it now. *Shame.* Shame left me embarrassed about the color of the skin God gave me. It started young, and I battled the beast through many seasons. I was ashamed of my body because I believed others were dissatisfied with my almond eyes and thick brows and the honey hue of my skin. My skin and story didn't fit into their world, and therefore, I—with my thoughts, feelings, dreams, and ideas—didn't fit into their world either. I was a minority in almost every situation I found myself in. I was unremittingly reminded of how different I was.

Whenever you feel like the outsider, with a difference you can't control, you feel utterly helpless. You have no way to get what you want. It doesn't matter if you try to ignore your differences. Others will point them out to you unannounced. It's a crippling feeling, being different.

It was true for me. I felt debilitated with my brown skin and broken story. I felt the narrative of my life being written without my consent, a narrative in which shame forever played the leading lady, never to be replaced on stage. The truth is, shame is a liar. She is no friend to the abandoned heart; she is only capable of destruction.

Hebrews 12:1-2 tells us:

> Therefore, since we are surrounded by such a great cloud of witnesses, let us throw off everything that hinders and the sin that so easily entangles. And let us run with perseverance the race marked out for us, fixing our eyes on Jesus, the pioneer and perfecter of faith. For the joy set before him he endured the cross, scorning its shame, and sat down at the right hand of the throne of God.

Jesus scorned and despised shame and endured the cross. Not the other way around. We spend far too many days enduring shame and despising the cross, our path set out by Father God. If we scorn shame, if we shoo it off the stage as soon as it makes its appearance, we will begin to understand our place as free and beloved daughters. We will be victorious. We will endure the cross as we follow Jesus, the Author and Finisher of our faith. The Author and Finisher of our story.

The Dance of Shame

I pulled my long sleeves down over my tanned skin and wiped my tears. How had I let this happen? I had been so careful to stay out of the sun. I already felt so out of place and there I was, darker than before. After hours in the Ford Aerostar, bound for a family camp in Santa Cruz, California, we spent the night at an economy motel. Eager to splash with my brothers in the motel pool, I knew the sweltering California sunshine would leave me with an unwanted tan, my skin wheatish brown.

We shed our coat of shame when we accept that He took on our shame, once and for all, so we wouldn't have to.

I wanted so badly to be white. I would've given anything to have the strawberry blonde locks. The hairless legs. The peachy skin. I swore to myself I could wear that proudly. I wanted to be white because I was convinced it was not OK to be brown. Other than my African American Barbie doll, I saw no one around me who was proud of her dark skin. I struggled to identify as East Indian. I didn't know a lick about the culture. At school, learning about national holidays, popular cuisine, and customs of the Hindu culture fascinated me.

As women, we find ourselves in the traditional female dance of body shaming. Why is that? Why is it that our hair is not straight enough, curly enough, soft enough, or shiny enough? Why is our nose too small or too big, our ears too pointy? Why freckles, why crossed eyes, why arm fat, why facial hair, why a flabby tummy, and for God's sake, why cellulite? These are the questions that consume us for so long. We can't seem to hush the earworms of shame. We stare in the mirror, wishing for a different body. One that is the right height, the right weight, and most of all, the right color.

As time went on I began to accept my skin color, my broken story, and the soul it housed. Still, for so long, I let others steal my dignity. They had no right to take it from me, yet I meekly allowed them to step up, take stock, and decide if I was fit to be loved, to belong. For the rejected heart, it can feel impossible to escape the weight of shame.

In the Gospels, we read of the woman who anointed Jesus' feet with costly perfume and found freedom from her shameful past.

Luke 7:36-50 reads:

> One of the Pharisees asked him to eat with him, and he went into the Pharisee's house and reclined at table. And behold, a woman of the city, who was a sinner, when she learned that he was reclining at table in the Pharisee's house, brought an alabaster flask of ointment, and standing behind him at his feet, weeping, she began to wet his feet with her tears and wiped them with the hair of her head and kissed his feet and anointed them with the ointment. Now when the Pharisee who had invited him saw this, he said to himself, "If this man were a prophet, he would have known who and what sort of woman this is who is touching him, for she is a sinner." And Jesus answering said to him,

"Simon, I have something to say to you." And he answered, "Say it, Teacher."

"A certain moneylender had two debtors. One owed five hundred denarii, and the other fifty. When they could not pay, he cancelled the debt of both. Now which of them will love him more?" Simon answered, "The one, I suppose, for whom he cancelled the larger debt." And he said to him, "You have judged rightly." Then turning toward the woman he said to Simon, "Do you see this woman? I entered your house; you gave me no water for my feet, but she has wet my feet with her tears and wiped them with her hair. You gave me no kiss, but from the time I came in she has not ceased to kiss my feet. You did not anoint my head with oil, but she has anointed my feet with ointment. Therefore I tell you, her sins, which are many, are forgiven—for she loved much. But he who is forgiven little, loves little." And he said to her, "Your sins are forgiven." Then those who were at table with him began to say among themselves, "Who is this, who even forgives sins?" And he said to the woman, "Your faith has saved you; go in peace." (ESV)

This woman found out Jesus was eating at the table of Simon the Leper (Mark 14:3). She walked in, ignored the others, and made her way to Jesus. While the disciples and Pharisees dismissed her life and actions as irresponsible, Jesus disagreed. This wasn't a high-society girl. Commentators and historians agree that she, indeed, engaged in prostitution. Some say she was Mary Magdalene; others claim she is Mary, the sister of Martha and Lazarus. This passionate woman approached the King of Glory, wept at His side, wiped the tears with her hair, and poured costly perfume over His feet. Who knows what she had planned for that costly perfume? An expensive ointment she probably wore.

Her shame—what happened to her and the life she lived—was laid raw at the feet of Jesus. He accepted her. Her repentant nature made room for forgiveness. Even more, He allowed the ointment she brought to coat His feet. No doubt, He left the Pharisee's home smelling like her. He wasn't ashamed to associate Himself with a woman like her. No shameful past, act, or thought separated her from the love of God made plain in Jesus.

Jesus of Nazareth welcomes us all. As we are. He welcomes us from every nation, tribe, and tongue. One does not have to be from the Western world or have white skin to be blessed. You don't have to live on the right side of the tracks to be blessed. No one has to be rich to be blessed. No one has to have a perfect start in life to be blessed. No one has to be the right height or have the right hair color or eye color to be blessed. Galatians 3:28 proudly proclaims, "There is no longer Jew or Gentile, slave or free, male and female. For you are all one in Christ Jesus" (NLT).

You, just as you are, is enough for Him. No one is outside of His love, His reach, and His embrace. We all make the cut.

Shame for who we are, where we have come from, what we have done, and what we look like will always convince us that God and His healing grace are not enough. It will always convince us that we are a colossal problem never to be solved. That is the danger of shame; its power lies in deceit and sour thinking. God, in His infinite kindness, longs to rid us of our disgrace by convincing us we are worthy and whole. We can see His handiwork when we speak over ourselves His promises of healing, mercy, and outright love. Anything less leaves room for shame to grow like weeds in a rose garden, choking out the immeasurable beauty of the Master.

Jesus is near. He's been there all along. He's present in our shameful moments. He aches for our brokenness. He's close to the forsaken heart, itching to rescue and redeem us from shame that is far too heavy for the heart to bear. Jesus came to take away our shame. We shed our coat of shame when we accept that He took on our shame, once and for all, so we wouldn't have to. When we lie at His feet, pour out our heart, and accept His healing touch, we can stand up and walk in freedom and peace, for shame is no longer ours to bear.

CHAPTER TWO

Doubt

When doubts, no matter what they are about, creep into our minds we can be tempted to lock them up and throw away the key. In some faith circles, to doubt is a sign of weak faith. I disagree. Doubt probes and pokes, curious about why and how things work out for us. It's not wrong to doubt, and ignoring our doubts hardly serves us well. For fear of accusations or shame, we may hide our doubts, reserving them only for our isolated mind, where they never see the light of day.

Suppressing doubt will only move us farther from the faith; addressing doubt might just make way for a growth spurt.

Doubt, a lingering feeling of uncertainty, finds us in our marriage, our friendships, our parenting, and our understanding of God. We wrestle with doubt, whether we're new to the faith or we've been walking with Jesus for years. We can expect feelings of doubt to play a role in our story no matter what chapter. We may feel guilt for doubting God and His ability, but maybe we have got it all wrong. Maybe more doubt might do us good. In our doubt, we can wrestle for God's presence and perspective. He isn't put off by our doubts. He is a capable God who won't be shaken.

We make up reasons why we shouldn't question things. We don't want to appear vulnerable or confused. We aren't looking to disrespect those who've taught us all we've come to understand in our faith journey. But sometimes it's exactly what we need to go deeper in our relationship with the Lord. Suppressing doubt will only move us further from the faith; addressing doubt might just make way for a growth spurt.

God won't be offended by an investigation of our doubts. He won't be threatened by us. He is the Creator and we are the created. We are learning, growing, and doubting. It all works together. If we press into our doubts we will arrive at a place of conviction. It is that conviction, those firmly held beliefs, that will scoot doubt from our heart, mind, and soul.

Developing a solid understanding of what we believe and why is critical in our growth as followers of Jesus. We can ride the waves of others' beliefs and faith for only so long. It's healthy to question, to wonder, to ask, "Why did this happen to me? Why does God let me suffer? Why do I feel like such a failure? Why do I seem to struggle so much?" Our doubts aren't to be ignored. They are to be investigated.

In Matthew 22:37 Jesus instructs his followers to "love the Lord your God with all your heart and with all your soul and with all your mind" (ESV). That's an invitation to pursue all aspects of our faith: emotional, spiritual, and intellectual. Each of these pursuits is not intended to be isolated endeavors but to work together to give us a robust understanding of the love, grace, and power of God.

The Compelling Truth

Although my parents took me to church as a child, the truth of it all didn't really click until middle school. A friend from school invited me to the church youth group she and her friends attended. I had no idea what waited for me in the multipurpose room of that country church. I had no idea my entire life would soon change as I sat in the church's metal folding chair. I had no idea the presence of Jesus would be made known to me in a way that would transform everything for me.

On that first night at youth group, I slipped into a dimly lit room, spotted my friend, and sat down. Moments later, a student-led band belted out popular worships songs—"Shout to the Lord" and "Did You Feel the Mountains Tremble?" "God bless the nineties"—and I loved it. I was used to traditional hymns from my grandparents' church, but I enjoyed the contemporary melodies.

The good news of Jesus can draw us in without solving all of our problems, but simply wooing us to believe.

Surrounded by other thirteen-year-olds with their hands raised in the air and their eyes closed, I was curious about how long worship like this had been going on and how I had missed out on it until now. After the songs came to a close, the young pastor stepped onto the stage and talked of the goodness of Jesus—His companionship and how He fights for us. The pastor sounded like he was telling the truth. He sounded like he believed every word coming out of his mouth. I was intrigued, and after that night I found a ride to youth group as often as I could.

Week after week, the pastor would share about the wild life of Jesus. Over time, the words he spoke, of grace and peace, sank into my belly and made a home. I knew in my mind that Jesus loved me just as I was, yet something was still off. My heart thought it knew better. My heart knew that pain was real, and my heart was convinced that happy endings weren't for me because mommies really do abandon their newborn babies. Still I kept going. The love of Jesus compelled me. It appeared authentic. So all-encompassing. So raw. So hopeful.

People like that middle school youth pastor made me believe the love of God was real. We all need people like that, the ones who love radically when it seems you have nothing to offer in return. The ones who extend a hand when you're spent. The ones who stand in the midst of your chaos and proclaim a gospel of peace. The ones who invite you to be the person God always destined you to be. This is what assures you and me that the good news is true, alive, and capable of fully restoring us. Capable of handling us with all of our experiences, aches, and doubts.

That is the remarkable beauty of the gospel. The good news of Jesus can draw us in without solving all of our problems, but simply wooing us to believe. It reminds us that this whole kit and caboodle is a love story. God loved us and longed for our freedom, so much so that He sent His only Son so we could walk in the fullness of God. Every doubt we have is swallowed up in the love and sovereignty of Jesus. If only we let it. Without conviction, our minds, hearts, and souls will be consumed by doubt.

Christine Caine writes in *Living Life Undaunted*:

> It seems to me that every single day of our lives we need to remind ourselves that God loves us. The enemy of our souls will daily and relentless bombard us with thoughts and feelings of inadequacy, guilt, shame, condemnation, insufficiency, insecurity, fear, doubt, and rejection. He is an accuser constantly trying

to make us feel that we have blown it so badly this time that God could not possibly want us back.

Satan wants to undermine our trust in God's unfailing, indescribably, and unending love. If he can do that, he will paralyze us, make us quit, and keep us from stepping into the fullness of our purpose and potential. The only thing that can ultimately keep us running our race is the knowledge that God loves us. Once we begin to doubt that, our very foundations are shaken and everything else begins to crumble.

I want to remind you today that no matter what you have said or did not say, what you have thought or have not thought, what you have done or have not done, what you have accomplished or have not accomplished, God loves you and always will.

Love is not only what God does, it is who God is. He cannot stop himself from loving us because God is love. His love far surpasses any earthly love we may have experienced. It is based entirely on his character, not on our performance. There is nothing you can do to make God love you less or make him love you more.[1]

His love is enough to lead us and heal us. It always has been and always will be.

The Resource Room

In high school, I spent my weekday afternoons tucked away in the church resource room folding bulletins with the receptionist. It wasn't my after-school job. I was there because I wanted to be there. I loved those quiet afternoons. They were my safety zone. I would chat with the smiley receptionist about school, dreams, and what I felt Jesus was calling me to do. She would listen. She would give timely advice for my sixteen-year-old heart. She would send me off with heartfelt prayer. I loved each and every moment. Her love was palpable day after day for two years. Those afternoons felt like a cocoon where I knew exactly what I would get and what I could count on. It felt safe to be me. It laid a bedrock of understanding that it's OK not to have it all figured out with all my ducks in a row.

Our hearts long for safety and solid ground. Something we can count on. The deepest desire of a woman is to be loved, to be accepted, and to be safe. Wherever the shelter of safety may be—a therapist's office, grandma's kitchen table, or a church resource room—I hope we all find our safe place. I hope we feel safe to say out loud the dreams and doubts that consume our hearts. They both have something to teach us.

In safe places, with safe Jesus-loving people, we can ask hard questions. We can tell why we struggle to believe Jesus' promise of wholeness and redemption. We can share our wounds without feeling judged or shamed. We can be suspicious of goodness without losing our religion. We can wrestle for the truth, all bets off, to find out just how good Jesus is.

The Lord will speak. If we listen, our hearts will be encouraged. He will point out a new way of life. One we can't imagine on our own. One that seems impossible. He spoke in the beginning and He speaks to us still. To elderly Abraham, He promised a son. To young Joseph, He promised dominion. To aging Noah, He promised his family would be spared. He is the Dream Giver. And the Dream Giver delights in us. He longs for us to live out the dreams as we entrust our entire lives to Him.

Each of those dreamers had doubts about God's plan, but they did not know what God knew. They did not see themselves as God saw them. Their doubts of God were only a mirror of the doubts they had of themselves.

Restless

Isaiah 61 and its message of freedom for the captive first reso-
nated with me when I was seventeen. I did believe freedom was available and was found in Jesus, yet I could not shake the self-punishment
of refusing freedom for myself while insisting on it for others. I did
believe the Scriptures, yet some parts did not add up. I could not convince myself that I, also, was loved just as I was. I felt I had to earn the
love of Jesus.

Too many of us do this to our weary hearts. We assume we have
to be good at something to be loved, even if what we are good at is
marching after Jesus. For me, His unconditional love was at odds with
the rejection I stuffed in the corners of my heart. He loved me, yes, but
only if I was a good girl.

---

*Whatever state doubts leave us in is neither
too lost nor too broken for the ways
of Jesus.*

Some of us assure ourselves God will only love us if we stay in
line. If we achieve. If we become something. Then we will be loved.
We can do that. We can stay in line if it means we will be loved. We are
persuaded by our doubts that He will provide opportunity, community, and most important, love, as long as we keep on the self-defined
narrow path we build for ourselves. He is our conditional God with
clauses and contracts we construct and then commit to honoring. If
we fall out of line we work to earn His conditional love all over again.
We discipline ourselves until we believe we are back in His good

graces. We chalk up the good Lord to a scorekeeper, not an unconditional lover of our soul.

As an adult, I've studied patterns of abandoned peoples and their
beliefs about love. For many, it is based on earning a sense of belonging. Abandonment caused my beliefs to be at odds with my understanding of the unconditional acceptance of Jesus. My soul knew
Jesus was for me. My mind had yet to be convinced.

I couldn't make sense of my restless feelings. I did the only logical
thing a person does when she can't process her emotions. I stuffed
them down deeper. I somehow convinced myself that if I ignored my
feelings they would go away.

Dan Allender and Tremper Longman write in *The Cry of the Soul*:

> Ignoring our emotions is turning back on reality. Listening to our
> emotions ushers us into reality. And reality is where we meet God.
> . . . Emotions are the language of the soul. They are the cry that
> gives the heart a voice. . . . However, we often turn a deaf ear—
> through emotional denial, distortion, or disengagement. We
> strain out anything disturbing in order to gain tenuous control
> of our inner world. We are frightened and ashamed of what leaks
> into our consciousness. In neglecting our intense emotions, we
> are false to ourselves and lose a wonderful opportunity to know
> God. We forget that changes through brutal honesty and vulner-
> ability before God.[2]

If we are to learn to love God with all our heart, mind, and soul,
then engaging our emotions must be a normal activity in our lives.
Whether we've been told too many times that our emotions are liars
or that we're emotional because we are weak women, it's crucial to
listen to the cries of our heart. We wouldn't ignore a crying baby that
badly needs tending to, yet we do it to ourselves and wonder why we
can't think straight. Our heart is connected to our soul is connected

to our mind. All of them are subject to God's love and grace. His healing and redemption.

To accept the mysterious love of Jesus is to open our souls to His touch. This takes time and doesn't happen overnight. Whatever state doubts leave us in is neither too lost nor too broken for the ways of Jesus. He is our Love. Patient. Kind. He keeps no record of wrongs. He is not irritable. He is never jealous. He won't give up on us. Never. Ever (1 Corinthians 13:4-7). He will meet us in our doubt, curl up next to us, and hold us close. He knows we're complicated. It's never a surprise. He can handle it. Our emotions won't overwhelm Him, trick Him, or hurt Him. We can unleash all of it to Him. He will heal us.

Journey of the Heart

After high school, with no money for college but a deep desire for adventure, I joined a missions team in England. Without many mega churches and mass Christian broadcasting, it was eye-opening to serve in a culture so different than my own. With no familiar youth group to give me the warm fuzzies, I sharpened my belief in Jesus. I trotted around South London to share in public school assemblies, host youth small groups, and organize after-school clubs for those curious about Jesus. I spent time with young women and men who felt forgotten. I recognized their angst, similar to mine, and together we talked about a Jesus who was pleased with our growing belief. We didn't have to figure it all out at once. He wouldn't shut the door in the face of our doubts. He would welcome us in. He would listen. He would heal. We'd be witness to His grace and power.

It's wild to think the Rescuer accepts us just as we are. It's simply enough to be with Him. He can handle our suspicion. It's no surprise to Him. We give Him room to be God. We give ourselves room to be ragamuffins in need of God's redemptive goodness.

We see His grace and healing at work in the ancient story of Mary Magdalene. The Bible gives no clue as to Mary's age, parentage, or marital status. We do know she was from Magdala (hence her name), a city known for violence and debauchery. Some confuse her with the woman who poured costly perfume over Jesus' feet, but many commentators agree that's not the Mary Magdalene we see in Scripture.

We can't go on with a shoddy version of the gospel when a true, vibrant, full of goodness gospel awaits us.

With a glimpse of her in each of the four Gospels, we get a quick peek of her in Luke 8:1-3 as she traveled with Jesus sharing the good gospel.

> Soon afterward he went on through cities and villages, proclaiming and bringing the good news of the kingdom of God. And the twelve were with him, and also some women who had been healed of evil spirits and infirmities: Mary, called Magdalene, from whom seven demons had gone out, and Joanna, the wife of Chuza, Herod's household manager, and Susanna, and many others, who provided for them out of their means. (ESV)

It is here we catch wind of what Mary endured. She had seven demons within her who tormented and tortured her day and night. I can only imagine that when Jesus radically and powerfully cast them out of her, she had no doubts of God's ability through Jesus Christ.

She had been rescued from not one but seven demons. We don't know how long the demons had been with her, but we do know she had ultimate freedom and victory when Jesus came on the scene. He had enough grace for her. He had enough power to set her free.

As far as we know, Mary Magdalene spent the rest of her life in service to the man who healed her. She supported His ministry financially and traveled with the disciples. At the end of Jesus' life, Mary was there. She wept over His crucifixion and was the first person to witness His resurrection.

John 20:1-18 tells us:

> Now on the first day of the week Mary Magdalene came to the tomb early, while it was still dark, and saw that the stone had been taken away from the tomb. So she ran and went to Simon Peter and the other disciple, the one whom Jesus loved, and said to them, "They have taken the Lord out of the tomb, and we do not know where they have laid him." So Peter went out with the other disciple, and they were going toward the tomb. Both of them were running together, but the other disciple outran Peter and reached the tomb first. And stooping to look in, he saw the linen cloths lying there, but he did not go in. Then Simon Peter came, following him, and went into the tomb. He saw the linen cloths lying there, and the face cloth, which had been on Jesus' head, not lying with the linen cloths but folded up in a place by itself. Then the other disciple, who had reached the tomb first, also went in, and he saw and believed; for as yet they did not understand the Scripture, that he must rise from the dead. Then the disciples went back to their homes.
>
> But Mary stood weeping outside the tomb, and as she wept she stooped to look into the tomb. And she saw two angels in white, sitting where the body of Jesus had lain, one at the head and one at the feet. They said to her, "Woman, why are you weeping?"

She said to them, "They have taken away my Lord, and I do not know where they have laid him." Having said this, she turned around and saw Jesus standing, but she did not know that it was Jesus. Jesus said to her, "Woman, why are you weeping? Whom are you seeking?" Supposing him to be the gardener, she said to him, "Sir, if you have carried him away, tell me where you have laid him, and I will take him away." Jesus said to her, "Mary." She turned and said to him in Aramaic, "Rabboni!" (which means Teacher). Jesus said to her, "Do not cling to me, for I have not yet ascended to the Father; but go to my brothers and say to them, 'I am ascending to my Father and your Father, to my God and your God.'" Mary Magdalene went and announced to the disciples, "I have seen the Lord"—and that he had said these things to her. (ESV)

Mary had doubts as she wept outside the tomb. The angels questioned her tears, and even as Jesus stood before her, she had to suspend her doubts long enough for her faith to recognize that, indeed, her Messiah and Savior rose from the dead. It was Mary who was the first to witness the risen Lord. It was Mary who was once consumed by evil spirits and reclaimed by Christ. It was Mary who was given clear instructions to go and share of Christ's resurrection. Without a doubt, she did just that. She believed in who Jesus said He was and what He could do.

Our struggle to believe in the unconditional love, goodness, and nearness of God demands to be reconciled. We can't go on with a shoddy version of the gospel when a true, vibrant, full of goodness gospel awaits us. We cannot go on leading others when we're wondering if God is good to us. We have to decide. We have to decide if the God of the Bible loves us and is good to us. Day by day we can offer a tiny piece of our unbelief, a prayer, asking that He show us His good-ness and His grace. It's a small start.

We can tromp through life with a false sense of self and ignore the deeper issues of the heart that hold our freedom. We can miss life's greatest treasures if we live only in what makes sense to us. There's no such thing as limited goodness when it comes to the vast sovereignty of God. We have to go into the nonsensical sections of our heart and beg for restoration one day at a time. We have to believe Jesus is in the habit of perpetual healing, perpetual grace, and perpetual goodness. Our journey begins in the heart, addressing every doubt that keeps us from living in all God intended for us. It's our doubts, washed away by conviction, that will lead us to savor both the death and resurrection of Christ.

CHAPTER THREE

Isolation

$\mathcal{T}$he roots of rejection run deep in our soul. As we try to survive it, it's not uncommon to find ourselves in isolation. Isolation is the outcome of feeling inadequate, unworthy, and shameful. In isolation, we disconnect from Jesus and people. In isolation, no one can hurt us. In isolation, we can be invincible. In isolation, we can be in control of what happens to us. While our attempt to survive is noble, it leaves us feeling even more rejected than we ever imagined.

We isolate to escape rejection, but in turn, we forfeit connection. We pass on the gracious love of Christ that is to be received and shared. Received by Christ Himself and His people. Our isolation costs us love from others that could point us to the redeeming hand of Jesus. A friend may be looking to lend strength to our heart, but we don't accept it. Instead, we give ourselves over to a perceived comforter: isolation.

A lion always roams, watching for the weakest of any herd. He waits until his prey is alone before he attacks. It's an effective strategy, one that our accuser has used since the beginning. Our loneliness is fertile soil for the enemy of our hearts to claim dominion in our lives. To twist the truth into lies. Lies that start as a whisper, but in time, turn into a deafening scream that becomes solid beliefs about ourselves and others. Lies about our values and our futures. His plan is to separate. To steal. To kill. To destroy our hearts. Not rebuild them. He has no good will toward us. None.

Yearning

At five years old, as soon as I understood the story of my birth, it wasn't long before I began to fantasize about what it would be like to meet my biological mother and visit the orphanage where I was left. I wanted to know every detail of my story, however broken and disjointed it may have been. I wanted what I believed everyone around me had. I wanted answers. I would visit friends and would see baby pictures on the wall and baby footprints pressed into plaster. I wanted that. I wanted a story without gaping holes, without unanswered questions. And so I isolated myself from others because I did not have what they had. Isolation was the result of feeling inadequate, unworthy, and shameful.

Wishing for answers to my own story would leave me daydreaming about the day I would meet my mother. I wanted to hold her and tell her I love her. I wanted so badly to snuggle up on her lap and feel her soft hands stroke my hair. I wanted to hear her voice, her native tongue, pouring out words of love and strength. While I knew my daydreams would never come true, I hungered for her, this woman who carried me for nine months, safely in her womb, and chose life for me. I'm certain she knew she would never see me again when she gave me up, but did she know that would be a loss that would shape my heart, aching over a primal abandonment that would only be healed by the Father who had knit me together and called me beloved?

My isolation gave me comfort because I chose the narrative. I was in control of my story. I was not offering it up to the God who I feared, in some part of me, may be responsible for my loss.

Brennan Manning pens in his book, *Abba's Child*: "Jesus says, 'Acknowledge and accept who I want to be for you: a Savior of boundless compassion, infinite patience, unbearable forgiveness, and love that keeps no score of wrongs. Quit projecting onto Me your own feelings about yourself. At this moment your life is a bruised reed, and I will not crush it; a smoldering wick, and I will not quench it. *You are in a safe place.' "*[1]

The desire to be wholly and unconditionally loved is fulfilled in the person of Jesus. He is the beginning and end of every hope in our hearts. This desire to be loved, that drives our every move, will never be satisfied unless we throw ourselves wholeheartedly at the mercy of the Restorer. He will be patient with us. He will handle our wounds with extreme care. He will not use the cheapest salve on our bleeding heart. He will be, as Manning said, "a Savior of boundless compassion, infinite patience, and unbearable forgiveness."

The yearning for a mother who wanted to keep me as her own would only be fulfilled in the grace of Jesus. I knew this in my mind, but my heart was trying to play catch up. I had no idea that healing would be hidden in the orphanage I wanted to visit.

Back to the Beginning

In my early twenties, after my return home from England, my job was dedicated to playing an active role in community development projects both here and abroad. My time in the UK exposed me to social justice issues that I wanted to help heal. Part of my job, once I returned home to the Pacific Northwest, was planning missions trips for members of the faith community. Not only did I plan the missions trips but also I traveled alongside others with a heart for the impoverished. At that point in my life, I had been on several missions trips but none as significant to my faith journey as the one I took with doctors and nurses to Kolkata, India. A beloved nonprofit partner to my organization served thousands of people every day on the streets of Kolkata, and I was over the moon when it was time to lead a trip.

As I was planning the two-week-long missions trip to India, I was also planning my own pilgrimage back to my birthplace. After serving in Kolkata, the team made the trip to see the sights and wonders of New Delhi, and I made the trip to the orphanage where I was left. I was able to find out the location of my orphanage by connecting with the adoption agency that facilitated my adoption. With an address, phone number, and date set to visit, I was ready to roll. Once I marked the date on the calendar, feelings of excitement and nervousness left me anxious months before I ever boarded a plane. My visit would be just a few months past the twenty-year anniversary of my adoption.

My suffering was real as was the glory found only in His presence.

Year after year, I wondered what it would be like to visit my orphanage, and the time had finally come to rip open a cold case. One with very few clues. I was twenty-two years old when I stepped off the plane in New Delhi, India. It was a dream come true. I hadn't been in India since I was adopted at eighteen months old. I had always wanted to return, so when the opportunity presented itself I didn't hesitate. I knew what traveling to India meant; it meant willfully walking into the mystery of my origins. This was my opportunity to find answers, to discover details of where I came from. Every question and every curiosity would certainly bring answers that would satisfy my loneliness. I was sure of it. I hoped to make sense of my story by returning to the beginning.

On a hot September morning, with my closest friend, Lucy, I approached the steps that led into the dilapidated building I once called home. With my heart beating out of my chest, I opened the door and, to my surprise, was met with utter silence. I expected noisy room after room overrun with brown-eyed children. As I made my way down a long hallway, my strapped sandals slapped the cracked tile as if their only job was to announce my arrival.

Soon after, I heard faint whispers of little girls chatting in Hindi from the top of a rickety staircase. As I got closer to the chatter, I passed bunk beds and rows of cribs. Beyond the bunk beds were a few little girls—heads shaved, ears pierced, staring back at me. Their eyes told a story of loss, but their smiles told a story of hope. Hope to come, hope against all odds. I had only a few minutes to chat and play with these young girls. I danced with as many as I could, their thin fingers held tightly in mine. We twirled around the room and erupted in laughter. Before leaving the room, in my limited Hindi, I told them they were beautiful. It was the only gift I had to give them.

After my time with the young girls, I continued to the nursery. I took a deep breath as I peeked into the cribs. Many of the babies slept while covered only in rashes, chicken pox, and who knows what else. Their chests rose and fell as sweat dripped from their foreheads. After a few minutes, they began to wake up from their naps. One bright-eyed baby girl started screaming, and I motioned to the caretaker for permission to pick her up. She smiled back at me so I took her gesture as approval of my request. I scooped up the screaming baby, and for just a moment she calmed her screams. She grabbed onto me, holding me close. After a moment, her eyes darted around the room, looking for someone she knew but never landing on a familiar face. Feeling unsure, she wailed until her eyes turned red and tears poured down her face. She knew something wasn't right. It was a feeling I also knew all too well. She knew there was someone missing. I knew she spent her waking hours waiting and watching for someone to claim her as their own.

Those painful tugs of longing had mostly faded as Christ made His home in me. Yet, I still struggled to believe that His love wasn't conditional, that His love would only be mine if I kept myself straight-laced with all my ducks in a row. I still held on to my deepest hurt of abandonment. I deeply believed it was my cross to bear this side of heaven. It left me with a continual struggle with deep loneliness.

My time holding that precious baby left both her and me in tears. She cried for someone to love her, and I cried for her loss and, somewhere deep in my own heart, my own loss. Soon after all the babies were awake, I was sitting among a dozen baby girls, all without a mother of their own, ready to nurse, to run her fingers through their hair; without a father of their own to kiss their foreheads as he snuggled them in a rocking chair. My heart was breaking. I fought back buckets of tears as each one reached her arms to be held, cuddled, caressed. Those darling babies wanted so badly to connect, to attach, to bond with someone who would tenderly love them. They felt so alone, and so did I.

The brokenness of each baby and the hunger for relationship left me with a flood of tears. My throat tightened, and tears stained my face. I could barely stand. It took everything in me not to find myself in the fetal position, weeping. In desperation, I laid my hands over one crib and began to pray. I believed Jesus was in the room. It was my only hope. Regardless of how these girls ended up in an orphanage, I had to believe Jesus was present and near to the destitute. They are not forgotten. They are not alone. They are not leftover. They are not trash.

I prayed and pleaded with Jesus to bring a sense of belonging, of nearness, to these orphaned girls, and I asked him to bind up the brokenhearted. As I was praying I was overcome with the relentless love of Jesus—a love that seeks us out in our most vulnerable moments, a love that promises wholeness, healing, and comfort tucked deep in his presence. A love that doesn't explain our pasts but instead sets us on high ground for our pilgrimage forward, a pilgrimage in the name of love, justice, and truth. He loved and continues to love the poor, abandoned, Indian baby girl who was left in the trash, without anyone to care for her, as much as He loves you and me. I know He does.

She is not alone.

We are not alone.

Henry Cloud writes in his book *Changes That Heal*:

> Bonding is one of the most basic and foundational ideas in life and the universe. It is a basic human need. God created us with a hunger for relationship—for relationship with him and with our fellow people. At our very core we are relational beings. Without a solid, bonded relationship, the human soul will become mired in psychological and emotional problems. The soul cannot prosper without being connected to others. No matter what characteristics we possess, or what accomplishments we amass, without solid emotional connectedness, without bonding to God and other humans . . . [we] will suffer sickness of the soul.[2]

No matter how isolation finds us—through parental loss, divorce, or broken friendships—it rewires our thinking in such a way that makes it feel impossible to belong to God or others. It leaves us hypersensitive, struggling to connect in a positive way with those we are in community with. It distorts our view of relationships. It makes it difficult to trust another.

Yet, when we choose vulnerability, to trust another, and to trust God with our feeble heart, we take steps toward courage and a healthy bond with Christ and others. Vulnerability is the offering of our raw and fragile emotions without any idea of how another will respond. Will they love us? Will they leave us? Will they judge us? We do not get to decide. Vulnerability with God and others is a risk, but it is one worth taking. Brené Brown writes in *Daring Greatly*:

> What most of us fail to understand and what took me a decade of research to learn is that vulnerability is also the cradle of the emotions and experiences that we crave. Vulnerability is the birthplace of love, belonging, joy, courage, empathy, and creativity. It is the source of hope, empathy, accountability, and authenticity. If we want greater clarity in our purpose or deeper and more meaningful spiritual lives, vulnerability is the path.[3]

Our rejection leads to isolation, but vulnerability offers a new way. A better way. An exchange that requires gumption to expose our soul. As we offer our hurt, piece by piece, to Jesus, He is faithful to restore us. To connect us to Himself and give us a heart for healthy connection with others. Vulnerability is not to be shameful or seen as weakness, but in fact, it is our strength.

Deep and Wide

The morning of the orphanage visit I had been reading Ephesians 3 and had never been so deeply moved by Paul's encouragement to the church in Ephesus, as I was that day. Verses 17 through 19 read, "I pray that you, being rooted and established in love, may have power, together with all the Lord's holy people, to grasp how wide and long and high and deep is the love of Christ, and to know this love that surpasses knowledge—that you may be filled to the measure of all the fullness of God."

A love that surpasses knowledge is sometimes more than we want to accept. For me, it meant that no matter what answers I hoped to find in the orphanage, no amount of new knowledge would prompt love for God. We aren't prompted to love because we've been given magical answers to life's questions; we're prompted by the Spirit to experience and understand the love of God. He gives us understanding and insight into the ways of Father God.

In relationships, we've been hurt and it is in our relationship with the Father that we will be healed.

Abandonment in my vulnerable moment prevented me from trusting that God loved me, but my freedom was found in offering Him those vulnerable memories. I asked the same question that so many ask, "Why does God let me suffer?" It was the wrong question. It took a trip across the world to carve the questions out of my heart and replace them with deep compassion and love. Romans 8:17 became my heart song: "Now if we are children, then we are heirs—heirs of God and co-heirs with Christ, if indeed we share in his sufferings in order that we may also share in his glory."

When we accept the love of God into our life it transforms the way we think, dream, relate, and love.

Everything I knew about the love of Jesus became mine to claim, mine to believe. My striving, my wishing, my isolation was all replaced with a Savior accustomed to my grief, one who draws near to the brokenhearted. He knit me in my mother's womb, held me at birth, carried me throughout the years, and set me free in the very place I believed He left me. Only God could do that. Only God could free me from the loveless prison I created for myself. No amount of willpower could ever produce the freedom hidden in the death and resurrection of Jesus. My freedom was unlocked by His love. His presence became the answer to every one of the countless questions I had asked over the years.

May isolation be a ship that sails far away from our hearts, never to return as we engage others in the hard work of honest and vulnerable relationships.

I may not have a clue how each of those darling babies will be cared for or where they will end up in life, but I do believe Christ is near in their brokenness; He will bind up their hearts, and He will set them free. Jesus will love them with an everlasting love. He will be their father and mother, and He will be their Savior. They belong to Him. Of this I am sure.

He's done it for me.

He can do it for all of us.

He will not leave us isolated. He will come for us.

When we accept the love of God into our life it transforms the way we think, dream, relate, and love. We want to skip over our aches and pains. We want to forget that through our hurts, we can find what we've been looking for: healing and restoration—a healing that can cast off doubt and a restoration that eases anxiety and fills us to the brim with grace. A healing that informs our hearts that we belong.

We can experience freedom when we take every isolating thought captive, the thoughts that tell us we aren't worthy enough, pretty enough, or good enough to be loved by a friend, spouse, parent, or pastor. These thoughts make isolation an appealing option in our lives. Instead, we must stand on the promises of the Father. The one who invites us to the table where we never need to fight for a place but are always welcome. Because we are children of God (John 1:12), a friend of Jesus (John 15:15), beloved (Colossians 3:12), a branch of the True Vine (John 15:1, 5), no longer a slave to sin (Romans 6:6), never condemned (Romans 8:1), chosen (1 Thessalonians 1:4), an heir (Romans 8:17), accepted (Romans 15:17), a new creation (2 Corinthians 5:17), forgiven (Ephesians 1:17), alive with Christ (Ephesians 2:4-5), a citizen of heaven (Philippians 3:20), God's workmanship (Ephesians 2:10), and a member of the body and partaker of His promise (Ephesians 3:6).

Love Heals

As the Good Father is patient with us we can be patient with ourselves. We can see how isolation has been our method of coping instead of the counterintuitive act of vulnerability. We can see in His Word, coupled with the Holy Spirit, a true understanding of why He came in the first place. He came to repair the relationship. He came so isolation would never have to be the final outcome in our lives.

Isolation from God leaves us suffering. Isolation from others leaves us lonely. In relationships, we've been hurt and it is in our relationship with the Father that we will be healed. As we offer our vulnerable experiences to the Father and receive His love and truth, our hearts grow stronger. Braver.

As we lean into the acceptance of Jesus we are able to approach relationships around us differently. We do not have to reject ourselves assuming someone else will first. We do not have to reject others before they presumably reject us. It is true that we cannot control how someone will treat us; we cannot control someone else's ability to hurt our hearts. But it is also true that we can choose who we share our lives with, who we share our vulnerability with. We can bear our burdens with one another. We can choose to overlook offenses, to offer forgiveness, to offer grace. It will set us free when isolation wants to wrap its chains around us. Galatians 6:1-3 reminds us, "Live creatively, friends. If someone falls into sin, forgivingly restore him, saving your critical comments for yourself. *You* might be needing forgiveness before the day's out. Stoop down and reach out to those who are oppressed. Share their burdens, and so complete Christ's law. If you think you are too good for that, you are badly deceived" (MSG).

Relationships are hard work. We are bound to hurt one another. We are bound to offend one another. But we redeem what has been broken when we forgive, when we offer our vulnerability and look to care for one another, nurturing the healing and wholeness that is set in motion by the Redeemer of us all. We must not let the hurt and pain from another define us while Christ has set out to do that very job. As we seek connection with others we will see communion at its best. A deep connection with God and a growing connection with one another.

Lending Strength

After my time in the orphanage, my dearest friend, Lucy, and I were escorted back to our hostel. We exchanged few words on the hour-long car ride. The day's events played over and over in my head. Once we arrived at our room I let out a sigh and started to sob. I laid face-down on my flimsy twin bed and let the pillow sop up my tears. Lucy, without the utterance of a single word, sat next to me and cried. I didn't need a pep talk. I didn't need bright, shiny words of encouragement. In my fragile moment, she mourned with me. She didn't leave my side. She was the hands, feet, and mouthpiece of Jesus for me in a sore moment.

It's a beautiful thing to allow another to lend his or her strength to us in our weary state. We may feel alone, but all around us, God offers us image bearers. To listen. To hug. To cry. To hear our story. In the same way, we dip our toes in the water and start to do the same. As we do, we see how isolation's devastating effects breed self-pity, emptiness, and insignificance. We see it in ourselves and we see it in others around us. We realize that we need each other to expose the heart of God, His goodness, and His companionship. We see the hand of God's healing grace, not when we wallow in self-pity, but when we find our lives satisfied in Christ. The opposite of isolation is neediness. It is hearty connection with ourselves, with others, with God.

As we break the chains of isolation we learn to love without condition and to care without expectations. We do not expect others to fix us or meet our impossible standards. As our vulnerability is safe in Christ we see it as strength with one another.

When we love others as ourselves we make progress. We see Jesus at work, uprooting and repairing years of hurt. When we love others with the same love we desire, we change the narrative of our story from one of loss and isolation to one of deeply grounded connection to God and man.

Let us work in our relationships, in our tribes, to let there be connection that is not defined by race or economic standing. By haves or have-nots. By put together or broken. Rather, let there be a common bond in faith, one that marks us as lovers of redemption and justice, truth and grace, hope and adventure. Let us work to allow this love to speak over our intentions, how we act, our shared language, relationships, and celebrations.

Let our language be beautiful. Let it not look to tear down, but instead look to build each other up. Let it invite honesty, humility, authenticity, and laughter. Let it never fight for position, for praise. Let it not spew slander. Let it be life giving. May our shared language stand as a witness to others how our tribe will not force anyone to jockey for clout, but will make room for everyone at the table as equals. No single soul is worth more or less; we will sit together regardless of social standing. May we never look to speak ill of others, spurring on the harmful work of isolation, but may love pour from our lips, gracious speech evident to all.

May our relationships be more than casual, inviting one another into our struggles, our hurts, and our triumphs. May we know the true hearts of one another, not just what we view on social media. Life is messy. Life is not perfect, but together we can work out our healing in the pursuit of wholeness while assuming a posture of forgiveness. We will most definitely upset and occasionally offend one another. Yet, in those moments, let us refuse to retreat, excommunicating each other. Let that never be our ritual. Where there is opportunity and willingness to change, let us reconcile our differences and divisions.

May isolation be a ship that sails far away from our hearts, never to return as we engage others in the hard work of honest and vulnerable relationships. There is personal healing available in connection as we are all image bearers of Christ. Adventures of heart await in one another. Even in the smallest of encounters, we can share the genuine with those we trust. We can build and deepen our wells of love and stand in amazement over a different outcome to our story: not one of rejection, but one of trust.

CHAPTER FOUR

Undesirability

$\mathcal{D}$esire. To crave. To want. The deepest parts of us that are fragile, vulnerable, and tender all hope someone will pursue us just as we are. Not fancy or cleaned up. Not prim and proper. Just us. At every season, a woman's great longing is to be accepted and significant. When rejection steals the true identity God intended within us, we're left wondering if we had any value to begin with. It appears as if no one wants us. No one wants our baggage, our story, our brokenness. The lies of exclusion knock on our heart hoping we'll open the door. Lies that whisper in the quiet moments that we aren't attractive enough, skinny enough, smart enough, accomplished enough, or good enough. To feel undesirable as a grown woman reiterates and confirms any feelings of rejection that have lingered in the lifetime of our souls.

Being sought after by another man will not fix us. Our lives will not magically change overnight if the man of our dreams walks into our life. He will not be our source of joy. Being pursued in friendship, while appreciated, won't solve our heart issues. Sometimes we feel that if someone craves us it declares our value. We act as if it determines our place in life. It doesn't. It never has, and it never will.

Prince Charming

He was dashingly handsome. Tall, dark, and English. My Prince Charming. He first caught my eye at a wedding in London. I wore a dusty rose dress that fell past my knees as I stood in line with the rest of the bridal party. He proudly stood in his charcoal-black coat-tails and bow tie next to the groom. After the ceremony, we found ourselves chatting throughout the reception. Unlike American wedding receptions that move rather quickly, English receptions move at a glacial pace. The ceremony began at noon and the reception came to a close at midnight. Needless to say, we had plenty of time to get to know each other. He was kind, chivalrous, and said all the right words. His thick black hair and ear-to-ear grin made me smile. I was smitten. Before we said our good-byes, we made plans to go out for pizza.

The next day, on a sunny afternoon in South London, I began a conversation with Prince Charming that I secretly hoped would never end. After two hours of chatting, which felt like two minutes, we devoured our caramelized onion pizza and headed out for a stroll through the park. We exchanged our stories, the good parts and the hard parts. I slouched next to him on the grass, drinking in every word he said. Our lives were worlds apart but similar enough for us to connect. I had witnessed the presence and power of Jesus from the pew of a charismatic church and he, from a liturgical one. In both environments, we found Jesus. In both of our stories, we discovered that Jesus wasn't done with us yet and that He would use any circumstance to express His nature.

My prince cared deeply about the things I cared about. The poor. The unloved. Those who felt hopeless. He spent his life loving Jesus and people. He served as a pastor at a church plant outside of Manchester and waited tables at a Mexican restaurant at night to make ends meet.

Like Cinderella and her prince at midnight, our time together came to an end. I finished my year abroad and headed home to the

States a few days later. I would have given anything to have met him months earlier, affording us more time in the same time zone and continent. While that would have been ideal, it wasn't my reality. Nevertheless, for the first time in my life, I met a true gentleman. The feelings of affection were mutual. I wanted to see what would happen to my life if we chose each other.

Before we could even decide what a dating relationship could look like, we said farewell. I wrote him a letter for his journey on the train back to Lancashire, about five hours north of London. In it, I wrote how it was such a joy to meet him. Even if nothing were to happen I very much appreciated our time together. Our encounter was a gift. Covertly, I hoped he would chase after me like every storybook ever written for little girls with dreams of a knight in shining armor. Later that night, after giving him my letter, he called to say we should try a long-distance relationship.

"Umm, yes," I murmured back.

I was certain God had heard my prayers. This was my big chance. My opportunity to fall in love and skip down the lane on my way to happily ever after.

The Scriptures of the Bible aren't just instructional and historical. The Scriptures are also a love story.

When we find something that looks like desire and smells like devotion we convince ourselves it will soothe our shaky heart. Our hearts, longing to be loved and cared for, are hungry for a deeply grounded love and will often settle for anything that resembles the stuff. A woman can feel on top of the world if she is desired by a man. She may feel that bad things can happen, but as long as she feels loved then she is worthy of value. We put our justification for existence in the hands of another.

The human heart longs to be desired. When it feels unwanted it can turn on itself. A heart that's beautiful convinces itself it's ugly, full of broken pieces, and useful to no one. At my core, I felt undesirable. I wondered if anyone would love me as I was. In my right mind, I would have never admitted this belief to a single soul, but I had this niggling feeling that I wasn't worthy of desire. These feelings as an adult, born in childhood, never settled themselves in the love and grace of Jesus. They ate at me; and I thought it was part of my permanent self, unable to be removed. The thorn in my flesh.

Unhealed pain leaves us fragile and tender. It confuses our ideas of what should be right in our lives. We're left with frustrated hopes and dreams. When something good comes along in our lives that ultimately leaves us in a heap on the floor, we find our heart in shambles, feeling a familiar pain, amplified. We feel as though sorrow follows us around, looking to strike at a moment's notice. Yet, the common denominator in our reactions to trauma, however big or small, is in ourselves. It is in our beliefs about our heart, it is in how we see Jesus, it is in how we see others, and it is determined by our experiences. We see the world through our pain and through our struggles.

A Love Story

Prince Charming and I did our best to keep the conversation flowing. We called each other every couple days. We scrimped and saved for phone cards, spending every spare dollar to hear each other's voice. I sure did love those phone calls. My eyes would light up when his name popped up on the caller ID. We'd talk for hours. All we had was conversation. No dates to the movies or hiking with friends. Just time to talk. To know each other's thoughts, beliefs, and dreams.

After a few months, we made plans to see each other at Christmas. I could hardly contain my excitement to see his bright brown eyes, tall frame, and toothy smile in person. This time not by chance but by intention. We were falling for each other and it was no secret. I failed to realize at the time that I had persuaded my heart to believe I was desired because of the person I was becoming and not because of the person I was.

We assure ourselves that if we clean up, stand tall, and be the person we ought to be, then we're worthy of desire. We're wrong. A man's desire for a woman is not rewarded based on a woman's merit but simply because she exists and this is promised to her by a holy God. The Scriptures of the Bible aren't just instructional and historical. The Scriptures are also a love story. They aren't about which man or woman was bad and which was good. They aren't purely a morality lesson. The pages of the story reveal to us a God who so desired His creation that He did everything possible to communicate His unconditional love, even sending His Son to express grace, peace, forgiveness, reconciliation, and wholeness to hurting people with broken hearts.

As I've served women in various capacities over the past eleven years, the biggest battle I've encountered is this belief, this lie, that we're undesirable. That who we are, what we've been through, leaves us as damaged goods, worthy of only scraps, never to be given a seat at the table of love. This belief is amplified by our ever-changing circumstances. As women caught up in this lie, we end up short on love, short on care, short on peace.

Heartbreak

After a precious time with Prince Charming's family opening gifts on Christmas Day and a stroll through the countryside the day after, I knew it wouldn't be long until we made plans to see each other again. I returned home sure of who he was, and I started to wonder what a life might look like for us together. Days turned into weeks and weeks into months, but before we knew it we were together again. He came to visit me and my family. We did what two good kids do and drank coffee as we explored our favorite sights. It was bliss. By the end of our week together, he told me we should consider our relationship moving forward. Music to my ears. Confirmation that we indeed had something beautiful, special, and unique. Something worthy of growth. I couldn't believe this was my lucky life. I was so dearly sought after by this charming Englishman.

We must be vigilant listeners to the beliefs, the lies, that are birthed out of pain if we are to lean into becoming the full, vibrant women we were intended to be.

We decided that I would move back to England, set up a new life, and live just down the street from him rather than six thousand miles away; and we would continue dating. I did it. I packed my life into two suitcases, waved good-bye to friends, and ran headfirst into a new season with Prince Charming, a season I'd only ever dreamed of. The first five weeks were full of double dates, searches for a place to live, and hunts for a job. Employment, for a foreigner, isn't the easiest to land unless you have a ring on your finger. After ongoing conversations with Prince Charming's pastor, it was decided I would work alongside him at his church. I was elated at the thought of serving with him. It was something we had only chatted about on one of our hour-long phone calls.

After about a month and a half, I flew back home to the States to wrap up a few loose ends. On the flight back to England it was odd to think I was headed "home." I had moved to another country for love. True love. A love that I hoped would last the rest of my life. I was on a one-way flight to Manchester, England, believing everything was in place.

What waited for me at baggage claim should have been a warning, but I never would have dreamed of such a possibility. It felt like it took hours to deplane. I passed through customs and heaved my suitcases off the conveyor belt. With luggage in tow, I scanned the crowd to spot my Englishman's curly black hair. I found him. He weaved through the masses and extended his hands for a hug. As he came within a few feet I noticed his ear-to-ear smile was replaced with a look of dread. I sensed hesitation in his embrace. Was he nervous that his girlfriend moved six thousand miles to be with him? That she packed up her life in hopes of a lifetime with him? OK, I get it. The nerves are real. His hesitation didn't shake my excitement. Not one bit.

Three days later, it happened. Prince Charming asked if I'd visit him for lunch after church. I bounced in, eager to be with the man I loved so dearly, and asked what we should eat. He sat down across from me and calmly said, "I have no desire to be with you." The words, within seconds, ripped open every buried feeling of rejection and abandonment that had ever weighed down my soul. His words were a trigger for a flood of pain I could not control. They were strong waters, too powerful for the dams I had built. I don't remember much after that. I did my best not to sob a puddle on the floor as I asked my only question, "Are you sure?" Through tears, and an unsurprising but sudden stomachache, I left his house and wandered the streets of a suddenly unfamiliar new city not 100 percent sure how to find my way back to my new "home."

I was a good girl, right? I did all the right things, right? I followed by the rules, right? Why? Why me? I just wanted to be loved. Desired. Why did this deep sense of rejection so severely mar my life? A birth mother. A birth father. The man of my dreams. None of them had been afforded to me in the ways I so desperately wanted. My thoughts quickly turned to self-pity and self-loathing. I decided I deserved it. Somewhere in my heart, this deep-seated feeling of being unloved convinced me once again that while God is good, He may not be good to me. These experiences produced a lie that felt to me like truth. One that I believed.

I spent the next eight months working side by side with the man formerly known as Prince Charming. The same man, who at one time confessed his love to me, had moved on to another darling girl who happened to be my roommate. Oh how I wish this were fiction rather than my actual life, but this was my true story, and I couldn't stop it. Each time I saw him it was a reminder of what I believed I didn't deserve. Even though my desire to be loved by a man was inherently good, it would never be love from that handsome Englishman I met at a summer wedding.

Loneliness set in quickly. With a grieving heart, I clung to Jesus. Through my tears, I would read His words of kindness, grace, and love toward the tenderhearted, but something was missing. My heart couldn't hear the comforting melodies of the Scriptures because the lies had a rhythm of their own, and they didn't miss a beat. I vacillated between feeling like I'd done something wrong to feeling downright unlovable as the person I was. I couldn't settle my heart. I couldn't heal my heart. I couldn't fight the anxiety or heaviness that found me—that finds all of us after a breakup.

Whispers

C. S. Lewis said, "Pain insists upon being attended to. God whispers to us in our pleasures, speaks in our consciences, but shouts in our pains. It is his megaphone to rouse a deaf world."[1] We may be blind to the wreckage that rots beneath the surface of our heart, but the Father will be present in our pain. At the center of our sorrow He awaits us. He will redeem us. If we don't identify the source of the pain it will run us ragged our whole lives. We have no choice but to listen to the shouts of God, who longs for us to walk in the belief that we're loved.

He knows we'll never fully grasp freedom if we don't identify our pain for what it is and what it's done to us.

He will find us, identify with our pain, draw near in our brokenness, and speak of a sacred way. A way of freedom and truth. A way of unity and grace. We must be vigilant listeners to the beliefs, the lies, that are birthed out of pain if we are to lean into becoming the full, vibrant women we were intended to be. Not free from sorrow but deeply connected to the Father as the Son reconciles us to Him.

When we see Jesus of the Scriptures engage with a woman's pain, shame, and rejection, we see glimpses of glory. We see visions of truth in a love that sets the captives free.

We see Jesus' beloved hand and heart evident as he spends time with the woman at the well described in John 4:1-30, 39-42:

> Jesus knew the Pharisees had heard that he was baptizing and making more disciples than John (though Jesus himself didn't baptize them—his disciples did). So he left Judea and returned to Galilee.
>
> He had to go through Samaria on the way. Eventually he came to the Samaritan village of Sychar, near the field that Jacob gave to his son Joseph. Jacob's well was there; and Jesus, tired from the long walk, sat wearily beside the well about noontime. Soon a Samaritan woman came to draw water, and Jesus said to her, "Please give me a drink." He was alone at the time because his disciples had gone into the village to buy some food.
>
> The woman was surprised, for Jews refuse to have anything to do with Samaritans. She said to Jesus, "You are a Jew, and I am a Samaritan woman. Why are you asking me for a drink?"
>
> Jesus replied, "If you only knew the gift God has for you and who you are speaking to, you would ask me, and I would give you living water."
>
> "But sir, you don't have a rope or a bucket," she said, "and this well is very deep. Where would you get this living water? And besides, do you think you're greater than our ancestor Jacob, who gave us this well? How can you offer better water than he and his sons and his animals enjoyed?"
>
> Jesus replied, "Anyone who drinks this water will soon become thirsty again. But those who drink the water I give will never be thirsty again. It becomes a fresh, bubbling spring within them, giving them eternal life."

"Please, sir," the woman said, "give me this water! Then I'll never be thirsty again, and I won't have to come here to get water."

"Go and get your husband," Jesus told her.

"I don't have a husband," the woman replied.

Jesus said, "You're right! You don't have a husband—for you have had five husbands, and you aren't even married to the man you're living with now. You certainly spoke the truth!"

"Sir," the woman said, "you must be a prophet. So tell me, why is it that you Jews insist that Jerusalem is the only place of worship, while we Samaritans claim it is here at Mount Gerizim, where our ancestors worshiped?"

Jesus replied, "Believe me, dear woman, the time is coming when it will no longer matter whether you worship the Father on this mountain or in Jerusalem. You Samaritans know very little about the one you worship, while we Jews know all about him, for salvation comes through the Jews. But the time is coming—indeed it's here now—when true worshipers will worship the Father in spirit and in truth. The Father is looking for those who will worship him that way. For God is Spirit, so those who worship him must worship in spirit and in truth."

The woman said, "I know the Messiah is coming—the one who is called Christ. When he comes, he will explain everything to us."

Then Jesus told her, "I AM the Messiah!"

Just then his disciples came back. They were shocked to find him talking to a woman, but none of them had the nerve to ask, "What do you want with her?" or "Why are you talking to her?" The woman left her water jar beside the well and ran back to the village, telling everyone, "Come and see a man who told me everything I ever did! Could he possibly be the Messiah?" So the people came streaming from the village to see him. . . .

Many Samaritans from the village believed in Jesus because the woman had said, "He told me everything I ever did!" When they came out to see him, they begged him to stay in their village. So he stayed for two days, long enough for many more to hear his message and believe. Then they said to the woman, "Now we believe, not just because of what you told us, but because we have heard him ourselves. Now we know that he is indeed the Savior of the world." (NLT)

In this exchange, we see a Samaritan woman and Jesus of Nazareth. It was extremely rare for a Jewish man to be in Samaritan territory, but Jesus made no mistakes on His journey. He was on His way to her. The timing was just right. He was there at noontime. Alone. At the heat of the day, she fetched her water. Alone. Most women retrieved their water in the morning to avoid the hot sun and the impossible temperatures of the Middle East. Yet, our girl is headed to Jacob's well. Some commentators speculate that she went at high noon to avoid others. She didn't want to be seen. She feared other women's comments and assumptions. But Jesus knew. She couldn't mask her situation and loss from Him. He was accustomed to her grief even before she uttered a word.

Jesus spoke to her, "Please give me a drink." She stood, stunned that he would talk to her. In the times of Jesus, a Jewish man would never talk to a woman in public, especially individuals who held such different beliefs, let alone lead a full conversation with respect and dignity. But He did. Our Jesus did. Why? To Him, her needs overrode any cultural divides of the day.

He didn't patronize her. He talked *to* her. He talked *with* her. He *listened*. As He explained eternal life with Him, she was baffled as she tried to understand what it meant to find living water. In her quest to grasp the meaning of Jesus' words, He asked for her husband. The

Lord didn't sidestep tender matters. She lived with a man and had survived five divorces. In a patriarchal society such as Samaria, a woman couldn't initiate divorce from her husband. Only a husband could follow through on a divorce. Whether she was a widow or left by different husbands five times, we can gather that she knew rejection. Even the man she was living with didn't make her his wife. Rejection marked her.

Jesus pointed out her pain and loss. Her divorces. He does the same with us. He knows we'll never fully grasp freedom if we don't identify our pain for what it is and what it's done to us. We have to pull up the root of why we feel so undesirable. We must debunk the lies and get to the heart of the matter, not carry on, ignorant to the cries of our heart.

The Samaritan woman, when confronted with her living situation and past divorces changed the subject. We have a strong tendency to do that, too. We begin to let the Lord expose what really eats at us, why we struggle the way we do, only to be overwhelmed by such heavy emotion that we rush to shut the door to our heart like it's Fort Knox. Nothing in. Nothing out.

Jesus answered the Samaritan woman's questions regarding the temple and eventually outed Himself by telling her that He indeed was the Messiah. She believed. She stood up, dropped her bucket, and ran back to her village. She beckoned the same people of the village that she had been trying to avoid. She told them about Jesus, the one who told her about her life with no hints or guesses. He was more than a prophet to her. He was, and is, the Messiah. Her Savior.

Like the Samaritan woman, we must let Jesus uncover the tragic plot twists of our story. We'll never be free of the sharp and amplified pain in our lives until we go back to the beginning and offer our first wounds. The ones that convinced us we're undesirable, unlovable.

We'll drop our water bucket and shout of His saving grace when we allow Him to love us as we are. Broken and raw. He'll take our forsaken heart and call us beloved. For we are His desire.

It is not a man, kids, jobs, or appearance that makes us desirable. It is always only Jesus. The Maker of us. The Healer of us.

CHAPTER FIVE

Lovelessness

*F*rom the moment we are born, and with our first breath, we reach out for love. We grasp for it. We cry for it. We have an innate need for meaningful touch, interaction, communication, and presence. It's how we were designed. We were handcrafted to be loved.

My dear friend Jana, after a painful divorce, said, "So, if love is what we all so deeply long for, then why does pursuing it seem to make such a mess of things? The very essence of our existence is built upon needing to give to and receive from others around us. But quite often, the sense of not being loved leads to a sense of desperation and disorientation that can spiral into destruction and self-sabotage."

The rejected heart is prone to patterns that hunt for wholeness. We find ourselves in similar stories throughout our lives, hungry for new endings. Our hearts are ravenous for healing. We may repeatedly date the same kind of man or carelessly run through friendships only to find ourselves frustrated as they unravel like a cheap sweater. We may look for a surrogate mother and father to fulfill in us the safe and healthy love that was absent from our homes. Our soul is looking for a fresh outcome but lacking the guidance needed to receive one. It is our journey for Eden. Longing for an unconditional love. Whole. True. Real.

A hunger for love can manifest in countless ways. If we feel unloved as we are then we will find a way to get anything that resembles it. We'll work for it. We'll hustle until we can feel it between our fingers and swallow it whole. We'll toil until our days are spent on what we could have had for free. We believe that if others are happy with us for our achievement or our beauty then we will be loved. Then we will be satisfied. Little does our heart realize, in our effort to survive, we are sacrificing our lives for a counterfeit, for a knock-off version of the real stuff.

Love is what we were built for, but trauma—whether neglect from a mother or father or mental, physical, or sexual abuse or even a more subtle experience—disturbs the image that God is building in us. Our true identity as beloved is chipped away, little by little, giving us the impression that we are doomed. Wrecked. Cursed. Broken. Poor experiences, especially as a young girl, affect a woman over her lifetime in disastrous ways. Trauma that leads to stress and fear is buried deep in our soul, casting a pall of suspicion over any interaction.

With a heart to be loved, I sought out friendships and mentors who would provide a different ending to the story of my rejection. I had no idea my soul was looking for a different outcome, but it was. I had experienced healthy healing with youth leaders and pastors in my teen years that began to heal the deep ache in my soul as a young woman. But after Prince Charming called it quits on our relationship, I struggled with a distorted belief that no one would want to marry me. All at once, I was too much and not enough. This life-sucking belief had followed me from middle school and high school. I was never the girl who was asked out. I was never the girl any boy doted on. The first guy I ever dated and had serious interest in—my Englishman Prince Charming—by his rejection, confirmed my growing belief that no one would want to make me a wife. A partner.

As a teenager in a predominantly white community, I thought my skin color disqualified me from having any boy show interest in me. As I got older, I was convinced it was my strong personality and outgoing nature. It was all too much. *I was too much.* Too much to be loved. Why then did I crave being loved so profoundly?

With a hunger for love deep in my bones, I could not for one minute believe I would be loved enough to be a wife. A mother. A partner.

There are too many of us who have felt this way. Too many of us have believed that we are not lovable because of our weight, color, wrinkles, or ankles; because of our lack of education or lack of charm; because we speak our minds, do not back down easily, and don't give in without a fight; or because we have baggage so heavy no man would ever choose to lift the hefty weight of it alongside us. We listen to the world, and our experiences tell us that we are ugly, fat, not smart enough, not attractive enough. We talk too much. We do not talk enough. We are too dominant and assertive. We are too passive and not dominant enough.

We believe the lies and live our lives according to them. We walk, talk, and engage others with these beliefs deep under our skins. We might never openly admit them, but they are there. Solid as cement.

Betrayal

I attended a young adult Bible study in the spring of 2008. I felt like a shell of myself the entire year before, still playing in my head, over and over, how things could have been different with Prince Charming. I thought I still wanted to be with him. I would replay the best of times in my mind, wishing I could return to them if only for a moment. And then it happened. At my very lowest, while I was working eight hours a week at a coffee shop and living with my parents, I met him. He was so kind. So caring. He ran in the same circles I did, and he always found a way to be around me.

It was crystal clear that he had an interest in me, but I could not, for the life of me, see what he saw in me worth pursuing. I told him that. I told him that I was not worth it. I was broken. I explained there was no reason to want to be with me. Little did I know that man would one day be my husband. The one I would work alongside to build a marriage, a home, a family. He would be the father of my children and my greatest support.

To know love — truly sacred love — we have to catch the unforgiveness that slithers so sneakily through our hearts.

While our love for each other didn't experience significant hiccups in the early days, my disbelief that I deserved to be his wife dug its heels in deep. Many friends and mentors gave us their advice and wisdom, which all came with their own preconceived notions, but the worst advice came from those we expected to support us the most. While sharing ideas for my upcoming wedding over pancakes and coffee, a woman close to my fiancé listened carefully and nodded encouragingly. She made me feel at home. Safe. I chose to be vulnerable as I bared my dreams and hopes of what could be for our wedding, our marriage, and our future together as husband and wife.

The very next day, unbeknownst to me, she and her husband called my husband-to-be and in their conversation listed why I was a bad idea, not worthy of becoming his wife. I was not what he needed. My appearance, my past, my personality, my dreams—they were all chopped up, mangled, and used as ammunition to convince him why

I was not fit to be his wife, let alone the mother of his children. I was betrayed. That experience tore my heart in ways that took nearly a decade to heal. It reiterated my belief that I was not worthy to be loved and any effort to find love would be futile.

Betrayal, even more than hatred, is the opposite of love. Betrayal preys on the openness and vulnerability you genuinely offer to another. Betrayal robs our hearts of peace. Betrayal makes us question if God is good. Betrayal throws us into a cycle of shame for naively trusting another with our vulnerability. Betrayal leaves us irrational, expecting to be double-crossed. Betrayal leaves us hungry for control. A control that will never allow anyone to hurt us again. A control that causes us to choose to never need another person again.

My response to betrayal was hate. Hate gave me control. Hate gave me a position of power that I thought I needed to survive and to protect my heart. In reality, hatred corroded my belief that God is loving to me or anyone else. Hate separated me from seeing love for all its goodness and transformative abilities. Still, in my hunger for love, I settled on hate. It seemed, at the time, the only response my broken heart could muster up.

Good Grace

To know love—truly sacred love—we have to catch the unforgiveness that slithers so sneakily through our hearts. Once we've wrangled it and identified those who have betrayed our heart and why, we have the opportunity to forgive them. Rather than withhold love to punish them for crimes committed against our heart, we can ask the Good Father to give us His grace. The same grace that He extends to us offers us freedom when we offer it to others. As we forgive others for betraying our heart, however small or big the hurt may be, our resentment loses its power. Grace comes in. Grace is offered to us in measures we could not even dream. For us and for others.

Grace does not stop with those we forgive. Grace is offered as we ask for forgiveness for the hurts and harm we have committed against those who have hurt us first. Against those who have betrayed our heart. As we learn to give and receive love, we will only be satisfied when we get to the bottom of ourselves and discover Jesus is our sufficiency. Love from a man, mother, father, friend, or mentor will never fulfill what was only meant to be satisfied by Love Himself. His love is enough to heal. His love is enough to redeem. His love is enough. In our forgiveness offered to others, Christ gives us fresh revelation of whose we are. He speaks over our hearts, claiming them for Himself.

We must understand that His love is present, but until we quiet the betrayal and forgive those who have hurt us, we will never experience the fullness of God's love.

This betrayal planted deep roots in my heart. My heart grew stone cold toward this couple. Years later, I offered the situation to a counselor. I could no longer take the torment of the lie. The lie that I was unlovable as a wife and mother. Every few months, the Enemy would find a way to remind me of this lie over my life when I interacted with this couple. I could not stand it. As I slumped on my counselor's burgundy couch I explained this hatred that clouded my belief in God's love. My inability to forgive had separated me from the truth. The truth that I am loved and that God's love for me cannot be removed by someone else's ideas or thoughts about me. I am loved. I had the choice to receive their cursed words and go on hating them, causing more damage to my own soul, or I could forgive them. While forgiveness is not a fresh concept, it is a powerful one. One that harnesses the ability to set us free as we claim Christ as our hope. He is the One who has forgiven us of much.

Through tears, I offered up my unforgiveness to Christ. The unforgiveness that locked arms with my childhood fear that I would never be protected, nurtured, and cared for. By God's infinite grace I asked the Redeemer to forgive me for every foul thought that had entered my mind and every loveless word I had spoken under my breath over this couple. Together, with my counselor, we asked the Lord to give us fresh revelation over this wound. He heard my cry. He told me I was enough. He told me that His love was not dependent on someone else's approval. I was worthy. He had made that decision long ago.

Our hearts, from the beginning, crave belonging and love. We challenge anyone willing to test our unloving parts. We give them our baggage, our pain, and dare them to love us. When they fall short, we are convinced that we are unlovable and that there is no God, or if there is, He certainly does not love us. We question His ability and tenderness toward us. We long for a love we can believe in. One we can clasp onto. We must understand that His love is present, but until we quiet the betrayal and forgive those who have hurt us, we will never experience the fullness of God's love.

This is the very reason Jesus came. Not only for the good, but for the broken. For the destitute. For the haggard. For the betrayed. He came for you. He came for your heart. He came so that you would know that not a day will pass without the Father reaching out to you by any means necessary, even sacrificing His Son. He built us with the capacity to receive love. Most notably from Himself.

Overachievers Anonymous

If love is free why are we working so hard for it? Why do we spend our lives pleasing others in exchange for the love of humanity rather than the love of God? In our pursuit to be valued, liked, and loved we forget we already are. Whenever we feel even slightly unloved our desire to be loved kicks into high gear. We work for what we have lost. We are drawn to whoever we think will give it to us. This can often take form in the need to feel understood. We want others to validate our choices to ensure they are happy with us. If they are happy with us and our choices then it follows that they approve of us and therefore they certainly must love us.

We feel a false sense of dedication when we live for what others think. We place boyfriends, friends, pastors, mentors, and bosses in such a high position in our minds that it seems noble to seek their applause. We use their compliments and affirmation as fuel for our fires. We, in turn, work harder and perform better. We love them for their approval of us. The relationship is conditional.

It's such an unfortunate cycle that too many of us get caught up in far too young. Our hearts are starved for the healthy love that mirrors the love of Christ, and so we seek approval from others. I don't believe any woman intentionally hunts for love in this manner. This frantic hunt is birthed out of great loss. It makes sense to us to soothe ourselves, so we seek approval. We see a clear path to get what we want. We know the work it will take, and we choose a target who will unknowingly become our counterfeit god, our idol for the relationship we want so badly, the family we never had, the life we thought we deserved.

Approval feels good.

I remember working so hard for the approval of another that I hardly thought of much else. I was in a new situation, but the same narrative took place. One in which I worshiped someone I believed could give me what I truly needed. What I really wanted. What would set me free. I did not consciously think that the approval of a man would mean so much, but subconsciously it preoccupied my thoughts.

By nature, I am a type A personality and I can get stuff done. That came in handy when I was seeking applause. With decent people skills and a keen ability to think ahead and offer new ideas to execute, I found myself in a position to garner praise for my efforts. I would feed off a compliment for days. It was nourishment. And I believed that if I kept working harder, thinking faster, and putting in the hours, then I would be the best and deserve all the accolades my heart so desperately desired. I was wrong. Instead, I found myself tired and confused, and my reality distorted. I found myself seeking the approval of someone I didn't even respect.

I simply wanted affirmation to wage war against the venomous lie that I wasn't enough. In the end, betrayal found me again. My vulnerability was violated and left me even more voracious for a love that was unconditional, not of this world. My heart knew God, but I sought Him in the natural ways of man instead of in the sacred ways of heaven. The entire time I had what I always wanted. In Christ, we find our entire life, the one we've always wanted. Yet, we keep searching the world over for what it can't give us. What it doesn't even have to offer. Significance, value, and acceptance aren't of this world. They are found in the death and resurrection of Jesus. Nowhere else.

We will exasperate our hearts as we seek approval from the men and women in our lives. We can spend a lifetime trying to keep others happy to ensure we feel safe and loved. It will never end. Our hearts will always lose. No one can offer us meaning and value like Jesus. He can be our sufficiency if we let Him.

We need the Holy Spirit, a great gift to each of us, to still our longing hearts. To give us a fresh revelation of true sacrificial love. A love that seeks us out at our worst. A love that does not demand that we work for applause. A love that finds us beautiful and worthy of pursuit just as we are. We need to listen to what Jesus has to say. If we do and believe His truths we'll stop searching for what is already ours. With the truth of God's Word and the revelation of the Holy Spirit, we will accept the truth that we are beautiful (Psalm 45:11), beloved (1 John 3:1), and known (Psalm 139:1).

Enduring Love

On my wedding day, my husband quoted Romans 8:31-39 to me in front of hundreds of guests. It was a reminder that my love was not enough. His love was not enough. Christ was and will always be enough for our hearts. For our wounds. For our mistakes. Every ounce of love for each other and others flows from that. He is the abundant giver and originator of love. The love that heals betrayal. The love that satisfies our need for control. The love that redeems our suspicious minds. The love that frees us from shame and doubt. A love that is fierce. A love that is strong. We will have the ability to receive love because we know Christ loved us first.

A love that is life-giving. Never life-stealing.

Romans 8:31-39 says:

> What shall we say about such wonderful things as these? If God
> is for us, who can ever be against us? Since he did not spare even
> his own Son but gave him up for us all, won't he also give us

everything else? Who dares accuse us whom God has chosen for his own? No one—for God himself has given us right standing with himself. Who then will condemn us? No one—for Christ Jesus died for us and was raised to life for us, and he is sitting in the place of honor at God's right hand, pleading for us.

Can anything ever separate us from Christ's love? Does it mean he no longer loves us if we have trouble or calamity, or are persecuted, or hungry, or destitute, or in danger, or threatened with death? (As the Scriptures say, "For your sake we are killed every day; we are being slaughtered like sheep.") No, despite all these things, overwhelming victory is ours through Christ, who loved us.

And I am convinced that nothing can ever separate us from God's love. Neither death nor life, neither angels nor demons, neither our fears for today nor our worries about tomorrow— not even the powers of hell can separate us from God's love. No power in the sky above or in the earth below—indeed, nothing in all creation will ever be able to separate us from the love of God that is revealed in Christ Jesus our Lord. (NLT)

Out of the love of Christ, we find true love. Not a counterfeit version, but the honest-to-goodness authentic love of God. As we pursue the heart of Jesus and abide in Him we find true love doesn't reciprocate hate but offers grace. True love gives and does not necessarily expect anything in return. True love leans into pain rather than shrinks back from it. It embraces the dark to search out the gift hidden within it. True love offers hope and power. True love is not scarce but abundant. True love stands with bravery and courage. It locks arms with forgiveness to unleash its healing goodness. It makes room for others and believes for redemption while claiming its own. True love is companionship with Jesus that gives us the grace to find freedom from every betrayal.

As my dear friend Jana says, "Love is oxygen and yet can leave you breathless. Love is a radical witness. When all was lost, we were never really alone or forgotten after all. There was Someone who was not just behind the scenes and waiting in the wings but was interacting, bravely and tenderly intervening, although hidden all along. This Someone had our good in mind and really knew the center of us: belovedness."

May the fierce love of Jesus drive you. Not your bad mood. Not your frustration. Not your disappointment. Love. True glorious love. A love that conquers fear. A love that endures. A love that has overcome. May love be your reaction and response despite what's been thrown your way. Love is far more powerful that we can even dream.

Beg the Giver of Love for His presence. In it is the fullness of joy. In it is sacred love that will soothe whatever ails you. I promise. He won't turn on you. He won't withhold love. He offers it freely. It's just what you need. You are not forgotten. He does not miss a thing. He is the very One who can stop the bleeding, administer the salve, and heal every anxious, depressed, worthless thought that creeps into the corners of your mind.

When our hearts suffer from rejection Jesus is the only One who can help us. Not a single human on earth can heal what was intended for the Son of Glory. He offers His presence when we offer our vulnerability. He meets us in our most tender and broken places. He will draw near. There are no shortcuts in the story of our lives. We have to play it out each and every day. We have to feel and face each ache, bruise, and bump. The hope lies in our willingness to question our heart, prompting honesty with ourselves and God. If we listen to the whisper of the Father it won't be long before we have the capacity to love in ways we hadn't before. He can illuminate our soul to reveal the hurt, bitterness, and resentment that distort our view of others.

He can point out the poison that has compromised our love, not protected it.

Whatever crack in our heart that leaves us hungry for love in a way only heaven can fulfill, we must unearth beside the Holy Spirit. The Holy Spirit will give us peace to believe that Jesus was present in our first wounds, in our first broken moments. He was not and will not ever be absent in our pain. He will never leave or forsake us (Deuteronomy 31:6).

The horrific events of our lives and the traumatic happenings that shake us to our core are not too far from the love of God. They are not too far from His hand, His ability, and His healing. He was there. He is not the source of our pain, but in fact, He is the hope deep within it. He does not sit idly by and watch us suffer in our loveless state. He is not the betrayer of our hearts, looking to steal beauty and innocence. He is the Restorer of beauty and innocence. He does this by giving us a new ending to the same story. The spirit of rejection is met with a dignified love that recognizes our pain. Christ will not diminish our experience but will lift us up and set our feet on solid ground. He will accept our despair and steady us as we walk in the fullness He set out for us long ago (Psalm 40:1-3).

CHAPTER SIX

Exposure

When we're exposed we scramble for refuge. Any rock or shelter will do. We are scared that we will not survive unless someone protects us. Although we may isolate ourselves within our own feelings and thoughts, we still long for protection in our rejection. We were built to crave protection and cry out for it when we feel most defenseless. A baby cries when it is scared. A girl hides when she is vulnerable. A woman looks for someone to protect her. If she is not protected she can start to believe the only one to protect her is herself.

When no one steps in to protect us, at any age, we either look for it in someone else or believe no one has our back. Our hearts whisper, "Look out for yourself. No is coming for you." It is just as common to look for protection in someone else if we have lost it from those we trusted. We look for others to fulfill what has been taken.

Even if we do not love our new "protector," we choose to shield ourselves in the protector's armor. While it may seem like a great fit, we are only fooling ourselves. We allow a man, a friend, a family member, or whoever else will give us a sense of protection to safeguard our exposed hearts. We settle for any sort of protection, regardless of the source. That protection may be coupled with codependency, verbal abuse, manipulation, shame, or guilt. If it feels even remotely safe or partially comfortable we'll wear it. We fail to remember, as my friend Harmony says, "Just because it's familiar doesn't mean it's safe."

If it is all too much we'll give up and concede to take care of ourselves. We deem the world too hard and too cold. The only one who can take care of us is us.

On a crisp autumn afternoon, I sat in a counselor's office and brought up an issue I was having that left me feeling rejected and alone. As the counselor asked pointed questions I began explaining my tender rejection and how I sought health rooted in the love, grace, and forgiveness of Christ. She empathetically nodded as I explained how isolated I felt. After some time, she asked if I had ever felt protected. I found it odd for her to ask, but I knew she was on to something. She did not insist it was any one person's job to protect me as an adult but asked me to share a time when I had felt exposed. Immediately my mind raced back to the beginning of my story. I pictured my mom alone with a baby girl, no man to protect or care for either of them. To this day I have no idea who my biological father is or if he is even aware of my existence. All I know is that he left my mother. Not a day in my life have I harbored any ill will toward my biological mother, but sitting on that counselor's couch, I thought for the first time of my father and his failure to protect her. To protect me. I froze.

Growing up, I had always felt I was on my own. It was up to me to make life happen. Forward movement would only happen if I took the steps. As I got older I assumed the best person to take care of me was me. I was my best safeguard. I could take care of myself. I followed Jesus and loved Him dearly, but I never thought my belief that I had to watch my own back was an issue.

It was not that I felt I did not *deserve* to be protected but rather that I did not think I *needed* anyone to protect me. I could handle any outside intruder on my own. After all, my life was not in any real danger. But my heart was.

My heart was not grasping the full character of the Father. While I hungered after His love, grace, and forgiveness, I failed to seek His protection. I failed to see its value in my life, in my story. I failed to see how it would unlock in me a deeper trust in Jesus over every inch of my soul, even from the beginning.

As the counselor explained the protection of the Father, I kept questioning whether I really needed it. We would move on and discuss a new topic, but I kept circling back, asking, "So, you are saying it's OK to be protected. It's OK for my heart to desire protection? Are you sure?"

She answered and then moved on, but I was gobsmacked. I was not letting God be God. I was not letting Him stick up for me. I was not letting Him protect me as a girl, adolescent, or adult. I wanted to stop at that very moment and rewrite my story. I wanted to go back and know a story full of protection from prey, from selfish choices, and from those I let take advantage of my heart. I wanted what was missing.

Our Protector

The Father sent His Son to save and protect us. I see this illustrated in Jesus' encounter with the woman caught in adultery. An ordinary woman crosses paths with the most extraordinary man, a man she had never met but who would change everything for her.

John 8:1-11 shares the story:

> Jesus returned to the Mount of Olives, but early the next morning he was back again at the Temple. A crowd soon gathered, and he sat down and taught them. As he was speaking, the teachers of religious law and the Pharisees brought a woman who had been caught in the act of adultery. They put her in front of the crowd.

> "Teacher," they said to Jesus, "this woman was caught in the act of adultery. The law of Moses says to stone her. What do you say?"
>
> They were trying to trap him into saying something they could use against him, but Jesus stooped down and wrote in the dust with his finger. They kept demanding an answer, so he stood up again and said, "All right, but let the one who has never sinned throw the first stone!" Then he stooped down again and wrote in the dust.
>
> When the accusers heard this, they slipped away one by one, beginning with the oldest, until only Jesus was left in the middle of the crowd with the woman. Then Jesus stood up again and said to the woman, "Where are your accusers? Didn't even one of them condemn you?"
>
> "No, Lord," she said.
>
> And Jesus said, "Neither do I. Go and sin no more." (NLT)

The Pharisees and the teachers of the religious law are trying to trap Jesus. They think they have Him. Surely there is no possible way Jesus can escape their clever plan to trick Him in front of the masses. In front of everyone, they drag out a woman who was caught in the act of adultery. Burning with shame, she stands alone. The man she committed adultery with is out of sight. It is she who is exposed. It is she who is vulnerable and bare, brought before those who have no care for her life. It is she who is to be sacrificed on the altar of shame. This woman, considered as low as a slave, is on display. The law of Moses says, in these sorts of instances, she must be stoned. While the accusers are trying to trap Jesus and use the woman as bait, Jesus chooses to protect her. First and foremost, He makes Himself the Protector to this rejected woman. She knows she has committed adultery. He knows she has committed adultery. But even so He protects this ordinary woman from the accusers. As for the ones who fueled her feelings of shame and rejection, He puts them in their place, reminding them of their own sin. He makes it absolutely clear that they have no place to reject her. To stone her. While we have no idea what Jesus wrote in the sand that day, we know it silenced the Pharisees, because one by one they left.

Our world will still ache in our present reality, but Jesus reminds us to take heart, for He has overcome the world.

He protected her first. Though she was naked and exposed, He made it clear He was not a threat but an ally to the adulterous woman. He was there for her good, not her destruction. His protection offered dignity. The Pharisees were scheming to make the scene all about Him, and He made it all about her, restoring meaning to her life and giving her protection and wisdom.

The Good Shepherd

For too long the world has shamed women, leaving them exposed. In biblical times women were as low as slaves, not even worthy to be acknowledged in a room. They were never to be approached, nor were they to converse with any man other than their husband, let alone the Godman.

It is the very ones the world looks to oppress most and expose most who Jesus redeems. He redeems the times we were left bare in front of those who took advantage of our hearts. For those of us who have been abandoned, abused, or unprotected from the enemies in our stories, we must never doubt the ability of Jesus to protect us. He can. He longs to. When we dismiss Jesus because we deem Him as the source of our hurt or consider Him unable to protect us from the accusers and abusers of our heart, we look to others to fulfill what we've lost. We pursue others to satisfy what only the Maker can. If we believe God has not protected us then we seek protection from others. We make small counterfeit gods in our hunt for healing. We want them to protect us. We want them to have our back. If that avenue of restoration leaves us empty-handed then we resort to our own hands and our own minds to protect us. It is a cycle that leaves us battered and exhausted.

When those who are supposed to protect us sit passive, our hearts break. Whether it is by a mother, father, friend, coach, husband, or pastor, we miss the heart of God when we're left unprotected. Yet, countless times in Scripture the Father is portrayed as a Good Shepherd. A shepherd's objective is to rule and exercise authority over his flock and ultimately to protect it from harm.

We see this imagery present in both the Old and New Testament. Most famously, we find it in the words of David in Psalm 23:1-6:

> The LORD is my shepherd, I lack nothing.
>   He makes me lie down in green pastures,
> he leads me beside quiet waters,
>   he refreshes my soul.
> He guides me along the right paths
>   for his name's sake.
> Even though I walk
>   through the darkest valley,
> I will fear no evil,
>   for you are with me;

your rod and your staff,
    they comfort me.

You prepare a table before me
    in the presence of my enemies.
You anoint my head with oil;
    my cup overflows.
Surely your goodness and love will follow me
    all the days of my life,
and I will dwell in the house of the LORD
    forever.

We are His sheep and He is our Shepherd; He is the One who protects us. We are the ones who are familiar with His rod and staff of comfort. He is our Good Shepherd because He laid down His life for us and we know His voice and follow Him (John 10:11, 14). Left unattended, sheep get lost or are attacked by predators. They are slow animals who are easily spooked. With poor eyesight, they rely on the voice of the shepherd to lead them along rocky ravines and cliffsides. They are fully dependent on their shepherd to protect them from harm. The same is true for us.

The poetic line, "He makes me lie down in green pastures, / he leads me beside quiet waters," is truly astounding as sheep hardly ever lie down or prefer quiet waters. In this comparison, David explains how it is God's desire for us to rest in His protection and care. We don't have to stand guard over our souls. God will. He will have victory as He leads and protects us, His sheep. We only must listen to His voice and trust His lead. It is in His presence that we will sit at the table He has prepared for us by His intention and grace. His goodness and love will follow us wherever we go. This isn't a promise of prosperity but one of protection, one in which our God is active to protect our soul as we listen to the call of the Good Shepherd.

Take Heart

Jesus is our Compass. Our Healer. Our Redeemer. Our Savior. Our Protector.

Sitting in the counselor's office that day I realized I had dismissed myself from protection. I had a wound of the heart and could not stop the bleeding. It never occurred to me that the very thing I "did not need" was the very thing that would move me from a place of rejection to a place of wholeness. Protection. I needed to recognize Jesus as my Protector. I needed to be able to ask for protection from someone else in my situation. My time of keeping it all together by myself would need to come to an end. I had spent far too much time trying to keep a calm in the midst of chaos. In reality, I was missing the heart of God when I did not ask for His protection, but to be honest, I didn't know at the time what that kind of protection would have even looked like.

His protection can look different at various times in our lives. In some seasons, His protection looks like someone else stepping in on our behalf. Sometimes it looks like peace and strength. Sometimes it looks like a closed door, with us never knowing why, but trusting He knows best. In His protection, we are never separated from His love. Not ever. His protection ensures His presence. His counsel. His deliverance.

In the Psalms, we see countless references to God's promised protection over enemies. Psalm 20:1 reads, "May the LORD answer you when you are in distress; / may the name of the God of Jacob protect you." Psalm 59:9-10 (NLT) tells us,

You are my strength; I wait for you to rescue me,
    for you, O God, are my fortress.
In his unfailing love, my God will stand with me.
    He will let me look down in triumph on all my enemies.

The protection of God is not about protecting our reputation or concerns. It is much better than that. It sets us up for victory. His protection offers us a chance to live from a place of victory. We have victory and peace in His protection. When we allow Him to reign supreme over our hearts, He will protect us. He will give us peace when it seems no one else will stand with us or root us on. His protection is not of this world. Our world will still ache in our present reality, but Jesus reminds us to take heart, for He has overcome the world (John 16:33).

Our Jesus is a gentleman. He does not invite Himself in and flip the room upside down. He waits to be invited, to be asked.

For the woman caught in adultery, we can only assume she craved protection. She craved companionship. She settled for a counterfeit. She sought shelter in the arms of a married man. While many would agree that was a poor substitute, it was even worse under the law of Moses. She most likely knew the consequences of her choices: loss of life. She fought for a place of value and protection with another woman's husband. I have no doubt this woman experienced such heartache before she made the decision to commit adultery. She didn't need judgment or isolation. She needed healing. She needed someone to stand with her just as she was. She needed to know she could live from a place of victory, not spend her life fighting for it.

This world is hard. Many of our bodies have been abused, neglected, and exposed to unspeakable experiences. That does not please the Father. It grieves Him. He will most certainly protect our soul if we yield it to Him for healing, for wholeness. What is eternal will be in His hands. Our soul will be His. With His protection, we are able to seek wholeness in our relationships, as we no longer settle for living in the place defined by what has happened to us. We can acknowledge that we are worthy of protection. The woman caught in adultery was protected by Jesus. We can expect the same.

When I beg for the protection of the Father in this new understanding that He is still in the business of protecting our hearts, I have found without fail His fierce and courageous presence presiding over me. He will, as we accept His love into every part of us, protect us. His love is retroactive. We can offer Him our pasts when we felt bare and unprotected, and He can give us Himself. He is a well of love, a treasure trove of grace, and a giver of healing. He can remove the sting of the past.

It may not be in the way we thought. It may be better. Deeper. Sweeter. There will be no more hoping that someone else will protect us; we will experience His strong hand of love. There will be no abuse, no betrayal. Simply love.

He has not abandoned you. He has not abandoned me. He is for us. He will stick up for us. He is not the source of our neglect. He is the Healer.

One night at women's Bible study, a woman approached me after I finished teaching. She was angry. Not angry with me, but angry with God. She said she could not fathom why on earth I trusted God. I explained that in my life every avenue of self-reliance fell short. I needed a Savior. I needed a Companion who would accept me as I was. A Protector who would hold me near and call me His own. I longed for someone who would give me wisdom and insight to make sense of my story. One who would not leave me to my own devices.

Unsatisfied by my answer, she questioned me more. She told me how her heart had been harmed and how she finally chose to walk away from that which she could not control. She could not understand how a good God could allow such unspeakable events to occur in her life.

This woman needed more than pity or a three-step answer; she needed protection. She needed to know she was not alone. She needed to know Jesus is there. Not absent in her pain. He is in the shadows, interceding on her behalf. He will heal and hold her if she will only let Him have an inch of her heart. Our Jesus is a gentleman. He does not invite Himself in and flip the room upside down. He waits to be invited, to be asked.

Abiding in the Shadows

We cannot go on living in constant anticipation that we will be hurt and left alone. We must exchange our suspicion, our distrust, for the ceaseless protection of the Father. With an understanding of the King as our Protector, we can ask for those in our lives to play a role of protection. There may be those who just need to know they are needed. It will involve health in the relationships around us. It may look like hard conversations as we set boundaries for those in our lives, as we share honest needs, and as we seek together the wholeness and fullness of the Father. It may look like removing ourselves from a situation that is unhealthy and hurtful. It may look like vulnerability with those we can trust. We must share our heart, if we want to never feel alone with those we love and those who dearly love us.

One of the many nasty effects of rejection is that feeling that we are responsible for the way people feel about us. This is a lie. We cannot spend our lives trying to keep others happy when we are alone with our hearts unprotected. We have to seek health in our hearts and in the relationships with which we surround ourselves.

A dear friend, in the middle of a meltdown over this very idea of protection, wrote this to me:

> You are not bound by shame. You are committed to freedom for your personhood and your family. You are walking in your redemption. Love takes away the power of shame to destroy you. Yes, it is vulnerable, but you are inviting a context of justice and mercy and disinviting oppression. You bear honor, grief, compassion, and curiosity. You are open to goodness. Shame is a teacher. We can respond to what it evokes. Your response is not to concede; that is not welcoming health. You have important voices. Upsetting the status quo is one of the most loving things you can do. Narcissism is not going to be dispelled by becoming complicit, but by firmly and kindly knowing you deserve to take space. Defensiveness will not change anyone. Only truth spoken clearly and plainly. Until you take undue power away from others you cannot bring goodness. You are not forsaken. God delights in everything that makes you truly you. The Word of the Lord for you is that you deserve the boundaries that beauty and protection provide. If someone does not have care for your beauty and flourishing, they do not deserve your time. There is a way to disarm without being unloving; reciprocity is the goal, but in the case of narcissism and abuse, you can claim your goodness and truth. Be grateful for how committed and thoughtful they are toward your flourishing, and if that's not true, you can fight

back by exposing that. In other words, you don't need to negotiate with people who will not reason, who will not see. The consequences must be addressed and they have a choice. The absence of conflict is not the same as peace or health.

When we have lived under the banner of shame for too long we forget that there is freedom available. We go on living in just a thin margin of what should be wide-open spaces. We allow others to have the power to reject us and to harm us rather than walk in the protection and fullness of the Father. We were never meant to be treated this way. Neither the woman caught in adultery nor any one of us. We are dignified and worthy of protection because of Jesus. Because that has always been the plan.

The enemy of our hearts is who will steal, kill, and destroy. Psalm 91:1 tells us, "He who dwells in the shelter of the Most High / will abide in the shadow of the Almighty" (ESV).

The shelter—a place of protection from the unforeseen—is found in Jesus. It is found when we submit to His care. We can abide in His shadow. His shadow, mentioned numerous times in Scripture, most always references His protection. With us sheltered in His shadow, He stands tall to defend and protect us. We commune with Him in the shadow. As He protects us, He heals our wounds.

Matthew Henry writes of Psalm 91:

> He that by faith chooses God for his protector, shall find all in him that he needs or can desire. And those who have found the comfort of making the Lord their refuge, cannot but desire that others may do so. The spiritual life is protected by Divine grace from the temptations of Satan, which are the snares of the fowler, and from the contagion of sin, which is a noisome pestilence.[1]

It's easy to sit from our perch and feel like others were given better odds at life. We find ourselves perplexed, frustrated, and confused by their seemingly perfect lives. The truth is, everyone is fighting a battle. Everyone is under attack. From sin, from others, and from the enemy. It is the same enemy who is looking to catch us exposed and to destroy the connection we have with the Father. It is a mission of the enemy to convince us God is not for us and never will be. Yet, when we abide in the shadow of the Almighty, we find the victory necessary to face the traps of the enemy and the hurts of our hearts.

CHAPTER SEVEN

Jealousy

We want her closet. Her marriage. Her friends. Her job. Her pocketbook. Her well-behaved kids. Her waistline. Her thick wavy hair. Her car. Her house. Her intellect. Her pearly teeth. Her confidence. Her quick wit. We want her life.

Jealousy slips so smoothly into the life of our thoughts. It is more than wishing or wanting, and it is far more dangerous to the heart than we realize. Jealousy, rooted deeply in our flesh, has the ability to separate us from our true treasure: our union with and contentment in Jesus. It's not always easy to walk the path of gratitude and contentment while wishing for more. As we strive for goodness in our lives it can be far too easy to compare our path to everyone else's. To see their seemingly perfect exteriors. All squeaky clean and bright. We compare our worst moments with her *(you know who she is)* best moments and covet a life that is not ours to live. We persuade our hearts to believe that someone was dealt a better hand in life.

We refuse to acknowledge what we know is true—that the women around us have just as messy and complicated lives as we do. "Nope. They're perfect," we tell ourselves. "Look at her, she has exactly what I want."

We often let our misery lead us to jealousy. We feel vindicated in envying another's life or season because we clearly do not deserve what happens to us. While we may convince ourselves we are justified in our jealousy, it never ends well. Ever. We label it competition or discouragement, but either label leads us down a slippery slope to envy.

We think her life, her treasure, is better than ours. Sparkly and shiny, everything we wish we had. What we relinquish is the buried treasure of our own hearts. In our jealousy, we declare that we aren't enough, that God's goodness is not enough, and that we'd rather be blessed with her story than settle for our own narrative.

Jealousy found me the way it finds most women in their twenties and thirties. I was jealous of the mamas. You know, the ones with screaming toddlers, designer diaper bags, spit-up on their shirt, hair in a topknot, no blush but a little mascara. The ones who claim coffee is a food group and talk about how they'll do anything to get their children to eat vegetables and not toot in public. Yes, those ones. I wanted mornings in Kindermusik with my little one and evenings spent cuddled up reading together. I wanted that life. So badly.

It all started on the beach in San Diego. With toes tucked in the sand, I explained to my husband how I thought we should wait another year before thinking about kids. He agreed. Within a month of our beach vacation we had a change of heart. We were ready to have a child. Pregnancy of the heart, not of the womb. We both felt strongly about the prospect of international adoption. After much prayer, we settled on adopting from Uganda. We feverishly filled out the paperwork, scheduled our home study, and began fundraising. We expected to have a little one in our home within a year. Many prospective parents at that time were able to adopt from Uganda within a similar time frame.

We envisioned our Christmas card with colorful faces and ear-to-ear smiles. We daydreamed about walks around the neighborhood with our little one snuggly swaddled in the stroller. We couldn't wait. Unfortunately, that was exactly what we had to do. Wait. Wait. And wait some more.

Our patience for what our hearts desired—a son of our own— was tested during the adoption journey. Having been adopted myself, I knew the effect adoption had on the life of an abandoned child. One year into the adoption process, we were informed that the little boy we were pursuing, baby Derek (same name as my husband), would never be available for adoption. In fact, he would be orphaned in his home country until he was eighteen. Thousands of miles away from the little boy whose picture hung on my refrigerator, I tucked away baby shoes and toy cars into boxes. With a barren heart, I questioned God, wondering if He had forgotten both Derek's need for a home and my desire to be a mother. Yet throughout my pain and questioning, God was so patient and faithful.

In the season when we were trying to adopt baby Derek, I vividly remember crying into my plate of pasta one night at a swanky Italian restaurant, wondering if I would ever hold my son, the sweet boy I dreamed of at night. It was that very same night that we received the devastating news that not only would he not be ours, but he would belong to no one. I cried for my loss, but mostly I cried for his. I believed this baby deserved to be in a family, and I desperately wanted him to be in mine. As we drove home, my doggy bag of $27 spaghetti sat on my lap. I couldn't eat with such heavy news about our case.

With my tummy growling and my heart aching, the Lord asked me to do what felt like a ridiculous and impossible request. He asked me to *trust* Him. He asked me to believe that He knew the circumstances of baby Derek, of my heart, and of my future. Over time, He revealed what I needed most—Himself—and that sustained and strengthened my faith in ways I never could have imagined. Although the weight of suffering knocked me off my feet and I felt as though I couldn't catch my breath for some time, God revealed His glory as He stretched me to believe and hope in Him even when I didn't see or sense His hand. Despite the pain of that loss, we stepped out in faith and started the process to adopt another precious little boy who had been abandoned by his biological mother when he was eighteen months old.

Why Not Me?

In the meantime, friends had babies. There were babies everywhere. I couldn't log onto Facebook without seeing another pregnancy announcement. At first, it was easy to cheer them on, but after twelve months of waiting I wanted my turn. My turn to change diapers and rock a little one to sleep. My turn to sing the ABC's to a smiley toddler.

"Why God? Why her and not me? Why does she get a child and I feel forgotten? You have forgotten me after I knew in my gut that You told me this was my next step. You led me here. You told me to care for an orphan and invite him into our family. You put this burning desire in my heart and now I cannot quench it." These were the plaintive prayers scribbled in my journal for more than a year. I questioned God's plan for my life even though His track record was good. I was filled with envy for a family I desperately wanted.

You are created in the image of God,
beautiful and strong, fierce and tender.

Proverbs 14:30 tells us, "A heart at peace gives life to the body, / but envy rots the bones." Envy will eat at us until there is not a remnant left of who we truly were meant to be. It distorts what God has done. It distorts what He intends to do. Envy is like goggles that only see what we think others have, failing to see what's blooming in our own lives.

Writer Andrea Lucado tells of jealousy:

> It shrinks your soul.
>
> Jealousy is toxic, yet we allow it to bubble inside of us until it's practically seeping from our pores. That sounds gross, but jealousy is really gross so I don't know how else to describe it.
>
> Jealousy is also a really brilliant ploy of Satan. What better way to destroy us than to turn us all against each other? What better way to stop someone's growth and prevent his potential than to paralyze him by comparison to a colleague or a friend?
>
> Jealousy stops you.
>
> You're plugging along, doing great and moving forward and then all of a sudden to your right is someone going just a little bit faster than you, someone who is just slightly prettier than you are or has a little more money than you do and just like that, you've lost sight of your goal, and your blinders are down.
>
> You're seething with jealousy.
>
> You can sit around all day and try to not compare yourself. You can try to keep your blinders on and be grateful for what you have. But when you start to identify jealousy as something that's attacking you personally, that's when you start to fight against it more. And that's when it starts to lose its power.[1]

When we feel jealous of another, we have to ask the heart why we crave what we don't have. Do we feel like we are not privileged enough? Did we miss out on the good things of God? Even when it feels like winter in our hearts and spring and summer for everyone else, our winter is still valuable. In winter, everything is hushed. There aren't the distractions of blooming opportunities and wild adventures. It's simply us and the cold. Us and silence. It can teach us something. We can lean in. We can throw our hands up in jealousy, frustrated by what's not ours, or we can find contentment buried deep in the goodness of Jesus. I've found that it's in winter that we see Him most clearly. Jealousy tempts us away from our intimacy and connection with the Giver of winter. The same Giver who leads us into spring and summer.

Jealousy robs us of unity with Christ because we are too busy wishing for a life that isn't ours to live.

The truth is:

It doesn't matter if you have been dumped, discarded, or divorced.

It doesn't matter if you cannot have kids or choose not to have kids.

It doesn't matter if you stink at house cleaning and you feel inadequate as a homemaker.

It doesn't matter if you cannot cook.

It doesn't matter if you do not make very much money or if you make a lot of money.

It doesn't matter if you feel too fat or too skinny.

It doesn't matter if you feel like a failure in your work.

You aren't broken.

You aren't damaged goods.

You aren't beyond repair.

You are loved.

You are enough.

You are created in the image of God, beautiful and strong, fierce and tender. Who you are matters. Who you are is enough. May you stand tall, shoulders back, lift your voice, and claim your inheritance. One of truth, rescue, and redemption. One of power, dignity, and worth. May you seek Him and find Him, the Healer of your hurts, the One who calls you enough. May He be your strength when you're weak and your fire when you're lost in the dark.

Contentment reminds us no one has it easy.
Suffering binds us all together.

This is not self-help; this is life in Christ. Romans 8:1 reminds us, "Therefore, there is now no condemnation for those who are in Christ Jesus." No condemnation. Not from your own feelings, not from those around you, not from the culture we live in. None. What matters is your choice to abide in Christ, finding your true identity, casting off all condemnation and shame, and walking in the fullness He has set for you. What the world and your own soul needs is for you to be most fully alive in Jesus. Not waiting for the scraps from another woman's table.

I have friends who long to be married. I have friends who are desperate to have a child. I have friends who would give anything to see their grown children return to Christ. I have friends who feel like God has passed them by. They grow jealous of others because they feel forsaken. Forgotten. It's the root of our jealousy that needs attention. Do we believe that Jesus can meet our needs? The emotional ones? The relational ones? The financial ones? Do we believe God is enough? Is His love enough to hold us? To make our story something beautiful?

1 Corinthians 13:4 says, "Love is patient, love is kind. It does not envy, it does not boast, it is not proud." The goodness of Jesus makes room for a love that is patient and kind in nature. Not mired in jealousy. It's our jealousy that gets us into trouble. It's jealousy that drains the hope right out of our struggle.

No One Has It Easy

Every woman in her right mind would choose a trouble-free life over a trouble-filled life. Hands down. She would be crazy not to. Unfortunately, that isn't the tale of our lives. Our days provide ample opportunity to envy someone else's life, especially in the impossible moments of our own.

Contentment can be the fire hose that sprays the flames of jealousy. Contentment says I know I'm not perfect. I know I don't have the desires of my heart at this point in the story. Contentment says I can accept my story, the highs and lows. Contentment says I'm seen by God and He knows my needs. Contentment reminds us no one has it easy. Suffering binds us all together.

Lysa Terkeurst shares, "I have learned that I am not equipped to handle what others have—both good and bad. I am, on the other hand, completely equipped to handle what I've been given. And the more time I spend being thankful for my life, the less I look around wishing for something else."[2]

Contentment makes room for us to be in sync with the Father. To take each day with Him, to offer Him our frustrations, our hopes, our dreams, and to carry on in the life He's provided for us. We see the priceless moments, the incomparable wealth, and the sacred communion that happens in the midst of our stories. He's working out a masterpiece within us. Jealousy leaves us hungering after a counterfeit version of the real thing. The counterfeit, a sordid god, is one that robs us of joy rather than lavishing joy on us.

We trick ourselves into believing jealousy will get us one step closer to what we really want, but in reality, it will lead us farther away. It isolates us, with our covetous thoughts quick to make assumptions about others and ourselves.

When we seek contentment in Christ we must give up what comes easiest: envy. First Chronicles 16:11 tells us, "Look to the LORD and his strength; / seek his face always." In honesty, we get to the heart of the matter, offering our sin, which so easily entangles, to a holy God who will meet our needs. Who will hear our prayers? Who has not forgotten us? Who is a Giver of good gifts? Who gives us strength to overcome? When we receive and walk in the gracious love of the Father we may rejoice in all seasons. His Holy Spirit gives us understanding as we seek Him. We accept the breath He gave us. He gives grace to celebrate our own lives and the lives of other women. Not bridled by jealousy, but vulnerable and honest.

Author Shauna Niequist writes in her book, *Bittersweet*:

> She [her friend Nancy] told me that when you compare yourself to another person, you always lose, and at the same time the other person always loses, too. Each of us has been created by the hands of a holy God, and our stories and the twists and turns of our lives, the things that are hard for us, and the things that come naturally, are as unique to us as our own fingerprints. She told me that one way to ensure a miserable life is to constantly measure your own life by the lives of the people around you.[3]

It's no use denying jealousy. James 3:14 informs us, "But if you harbor bitter envy and selfish ambition in your hearts, do not boast about it or deny the truth." Confession of our sin must happen for our hearts to grow out of jealousy rooted in feelings of insecurity. Jealousy squelches love. It promotes shame and self-pity. It cuts us off from the very love that's ours to claim. In our surrender, a counterintuitive act, we find healing. We find contentment.

In relationships, we may have been wounded, and it is in relationships that we will experience our healing and freedom. We will grow to bear one another's burdens rather than to envy the juicy parts of her story. Jealousy isolates but contentment gathers.

Kindred Spirits

In vibrant and grace-filled relationships we share our hurts, sins, and burdens. We hold each other accountable and seek Christ to fulfill our every need. We echo love, the honest truth, and encouragement for the road ahead. We see our friends for who they are, for who God is making them to be, and we find our role in their lives. We mourn. We cry. We lament over losses. In the same vulnerability, we rejoice. We cheer. We celebrate the victories.

We address our rejection head-on by pursuing healthy relationships, void of jealousy. We seek a girlfriend not to be our everything but to be our kindred spirit. To be one who we can share our lives with. We don't envy at a distance but offer up our vulnerability as she offers up her own.

A vivid way the Lord has shown Himself to me is through my dearest friend, Lucy (same Lucy who traveled to my orphanage with me). I met Lucy twelve years ago. She walked into a nightclub-turned-church in Manchester, England, with her strawberry-blonde locks and cobalt-blue sweatshirt. I missed home and was contemplating booking a ticket back to the States. Her soft voice coupled with her sweet demeanor was a welcomed gift to my frazzled start in England. She has this way about her, a carefree, beautiful, meek presence. She is truly one of the kindest people I have ever met. Her love was strong.

Lucy and I worked side by side planning school assemblies and faith gatherings for high schoolers. In between work we strolled through museums, spent hours at cafes, and roamed around Covent Garden and Hyde Park. One weekend we snuck away to the north of

France to cook duck a l'orange in a cozy cottage with friends. We spent hours talking at our favorite pizza place, or we sat at a roadside pub sharing stories. We laughed, cried, and had a feeling we were always supposed to meet. That we were always supposed to love and encourage each other. Proverbs 27:9 says, "A sweet friendship refreshes the soul" (MSG).

I'm convinced we are refreshed with kindred spirits because we learn how to serve them in their most broken and anxious moments, as well as in the best moments of their lives. They serve us in our most broken and anxious moments, as well as in the best moments of our lives.

All of our friends are teachers. Their own lives and loves provide a wealth of knowledge.

We both listened and did our best to comfort each other through breakups. In fact, when Prince Charming called it quits, she was on the next train out of Canterbury (six hours south of Manchester) to be with me. She stayed with me for three days and listened to me blabber on about loneliness and love lost. When she broke up with her American boyfriend and eventually met her husband, I cheered her on every step of the way.

At my wedding, she stood by my side. At her wedding, I proudly stood by hers. We threatened death to the other's husband if he didn't love her the way she deserved. Through the adoption process, pregnancies, dream jobs, job changes, and ministry, it's been an absolute delight to share life alongside her. Never mind that we're six thousand miles apart. Today, we each have two children, sleepless nights, stretch marks, and mortgages. A far cry from our wild adventures gallivanting across London.

Lucy was the first friend in my life I never questioned. I never questioned if she'd hurt me. I loved her for who she was. Not who she could be to me. She didn't exist to fill a space in my heart that only Christ could fill. At the same time, she most certainly blessed me in friendship. Together, over the past twelve years, we've shared our insecurities and our jealousies, and we have confessed our sins to each other. It seems when we spoke our envies out loud to each other they lost their lustrous powers. We've sought Christ's power and strength for each other, believing He's doing a great work within each of us.

All of our friends are teachers. Their own lives and loves provide a wealth of knowledge. As they serve Christ and abide in His love, we can learn from their rhythms of forgiveness, honesty, and repentance.

Friendship, one void of envy, is a rare rose. Cultivate it; sow into it. Believe the world for the other. Let your stories become interwoven into the tapestry of the kingdom. It will be something beautiful. United. Honest. A picture of the body. Not jealous of another but working in harmony.

Let's comfort each other and draw near. Not jockeying or competing to be the best. Not dejected over another's gifts, whether it be her marriage, her children, her season, her ability, or her influence. May we receive and be the manifestation of peace and joy in relationships when we choose contentment over envy and friendship over isolation.

We aren't a cheap toy to be replaced or thrown out with tomorrow's trash. We are valuable, one of a kind, not second best, but a prized possession. Ephesians 2:10 reminds us, "For we are God's masterpiece. He has created us anew in Christ Jesus, so we can do the good things he planned for us long ago" (NLT).

We were created to do good things because we are worthy. The good things of the Father are almost always rooted in healthy relationships. In our relationships, we experience the character and nature of God. We discover more of who we are, not less. We can see not what we lack but what we have. What we possess is a gift to our own hearts and a gift to others.

Equals at the Table

My wishing and wanting to be a mama, like so many friends around me were, left me green with envy. Like most in my shoes, I avoided any conversation that led to the question of why I wasn't pregnant or why we would adopt first. Once they discovered we chose to adopt first simply because we felt prompted to do so, they'd follow up with, "Don't you want your own first?" After I awarded them with my canned response they'd ask why we didn't pursue domestic adoption. They assumed that was best. "Take care of our own first," they'd say. After eighteen months of a paper pregnancy, my uterus and adoption time line were no longer up for discussion. It was all too much. Hear me now, I was graceful with my answers in the beginning; but by the end, my grace tank for questions from well-intentioned strangers and acquaintances was low.

My envy of mamas, with babies strapped in their Bjorns, wasn't what God wanted for me. If His plan is good it starts with His heart. A heart that is gracious and faithful. One that has a plan better than mine. In my jealous heart, I confessed that I had succumbed to sin that robbed me blind. It trashed my ability to see God work out every detail of my tricky time line. Only in my confession and surrender did I find the freedom to wait well.

I found the Great I AM. The I AM who is with me. The I AM who prepares a way and promises His presence. Psalm 27:14 tells us,

> Wait for the LORD;
>> be strong, and let your heart take courage;
>> wait for the LORD! (ESV)

In our waiting, we find that He shapes us to be the person we ought to be for what lies ahead. We might not be able to handle it otherwise. There's tremendous growth needed to walk in all He has for us. Jealousies only poke holes in our maturity rather than prepare us for the life He has destined for us.

I was a mother with a baby on the way. My time was coming, but my waiting indicated how much I needed Jesus. I couldn't do this without Him. His plan gives us an opportunity to need Him. To depend on Him. To listen to Him. He isn't torturing us by withholding all that we want. He is building us. Preparing us. Teaching us to wait well.

The friends I thought had it all fought battles of their own that I chose to ignore. Battles in their marriage, their work, their friendships, and their health. Now I was an advocate for their growth and victory. I prayed and pleaded with the Father to work on their behalf. I cried with them. Rejoiced with them. They did the same. We dropped to our knees every time we needed a miracle to be united with our son. I found a great gift when I surrendered jealousy. One that would have been lost otherwise.

Let's look for the best in others and the best in us. Let's celebrate, partake with, and learn from the women around us. Their stories illuminate our God. Jealousy makes us crazy. Before we know it, we think everyone is prettier and wealthier, more fertile and more put together than we are. It's a lie. Lies have no foundation. Even if others have what we want, we are still equals at the table. We can spend our days jealous of other women's lives, or we can savor the story of our own life, complete with its own bag of triumphs and defeats. We can be the women God intended if we will cast off jealousy and search His face. In His presence, we get a glimpse of the women He is fashioning us to be. Strong. Humble. Grounded. Faithful.

CHAPTER EIGHT

Faithlessness

We lose our faith in the absence of justice. When the events of our lives offer no obvious benefits to our hearts. When we think God should have intervened for us, protected us, or changed the outcome of our stories. When we can't possibly follow along with His unpredictable plan for our lives, we settle for the solace of disbelief. It appears to be the safest option after the baby dies, after the divorce is final, after the job is lost, or after a friend commits suicide. Disbelief in God makes more sense to us than believing in a God who would allow the terrible. The thought that God chooses not to protect us or abandons us in our hour of despair leaves our hearts unhinged. We can't bear it. Therefore, God must not exist.

God is faithful. He is not bound to us by a contract. He offers us a covenant. One that seeks and loves us even when we throw our hands up and try to back away.

For many of us, we don't wake up one morning and decide to walk away from the faith. It's a slow divide. We start with a bit of worry, a restlessness. That builds over time and eventually we have lost our resolve to trust Him. We give ourselves countless reasons to explain why He isn't good enough. Why He isn't able to fix our brokenness. At our darkest, we persuade our hearts to believe He isn't even there.

We take a wrong turn when we choose to worry about what we can't control. Worry is worship's enemy. Worry consumes our best energy for what could be the worst of our lives. It weakens our prayers and amplifies our limitations. It strangles our faith until we are out of breath. Worry makes us feel oddly productive because it feels like activity. We want answers. We think worry will lead us to them. We want to worry our way into an outcome, but we lose the one thing that can set our ship straight. Our faith.

God is faithful. He is not bound to us by a contract. He offers us a covenant. One that seeks and loves us even when we throw our hands up and try to back away. His faithfulness is His greatest gift. We may not approve of His perceived absence, but we must never forget He is always there, even if it is in the shadows, and He is always working on our behalf. For our good.

Second Timothy 2:13 reminds us:

> If we are faithless,
> He remains faithful;
> He cannot deny Himself. (NKJV)

Timothy explains that when we stick it out, when we grip tightly to hope, God can show Himself faithful to us even if we start to falter. By covenant, He will stay faithful when the sky grows dark. When the wind blows. When the rains come. He will be faithful no matter how severe the storm.

C. S. Lewis says of faith:

> [To have Faith in Christ] means, of course, trying to do all that
> He says. There would be no sense in saying you trusted a person

if you would not take his advice. Thus if you have really handed yourself over to Him, it must follow that you are trying to obey Him. But trying in a new way, a less worried way. Not doing these things in order to be saved, but because He has begun to save you already. Not hoping to get to Heaven as a reward for your actions, but inevitably wanting to act in a certain way because a first faint gleam of Heaven is already inside you.[1]

Our worship is an overflow of Christ's love at work in our lives. It expresses our adoration, loyalty, and belief in the character of God made evident through Jesus. Our worship, in spirit and in truth (John 4:23-24), sets us apart as people of undaunted faith. Worship makes room in our minds and hearts for the majesty and graciousness only Christ possesses. It is honor with extravagant love and extreme submission.[2]

Family of Four

Having no children of our own, we longed to be parents and felt this was God's desire for us. Despite the pain of losing our referral for baby Derek, we made a second attempt to adopt a child, a little boy who was left at eighteen months and had been living in a baby home in Uganda for about a year. With the adoption paperwork sent off and the reality of becoming a mother to a two-year-old setting in, I started to panic. Could I do this? Could I really care for a traumatized child? Could I, once an orphan myself, offer this child what he needed most? Would he have my same baggage? Shame? The same sense of rejection? Could God heal him? Could the Good Lord protect his heart? I sure hoped so.

In the frigid cold of January, the phone rang. The caller ID popped up with a long-distance number. It was our liaison with the baby home in Uganda whom we were working with. She asked us to consider the adoption of two children rather than one. I was daunted, excited, and nervous all at the same time. I was a little bit concerned by the thought of raising two boys when I hadn't even had the experience of raising one. I was nervous about screwing up not just one kid but two. Two pairs of brown eyes. Two souls. Two stories. But I was also excited, and my husband was ecstatic. He had wanted to pursue two children from the start. After soul-searching prayer, it was decided. We hoped and expected for not one but two children. We amended the paperwork to reflect our decision a couple weeks later.

Four months later, Derek and I boarded a plane to Kampala, Uganda. What was true in our hearts would finally be true in reality. We would be the parents of two little boys. After nearly two years of waiting, it was time. No more sleepless nights wondering when it would be over. No more worrying if we'd ever meet them. Everything from here would be smooth sailing, right?

We arrived in Uganda around midnight on Easter Sunday. With enough bags to fill two carts, since we knew we had to stay a minimum of three weeks, we made our way outside and into a sudden downpour. After thirty minutes of scrambling to figure out where to go, our driver arrived to pick us up. It had been a grueling trip, and the half-hour drive to our guesthouse felt like an eternity as both Derek and I fought off drooping eyelids long enough to get to our beds. Later that night, I found myself wide awake, tossing and turning to the hum of the fan above me. I couldn't wait to meet two very special little boys. Two little boys who presumably had no idea they were about to meet a woman who prayed for them more than seven thousand miles away.

After hardly sleeping at all, I finally got up and slipped on a cotton dress. The sticky heat turned my once silky hair into a frizzy disaster. I did my best to tame it and joined Derek for breakfast. We barely touched our fried eggs, toast, and bananas. How could I focus on breakfast when I was about to meet my sons?

Just after 9:00 a.m. they arrived. I heard the coos and babbles of two little boys. We started the video rolling so we could capture it all. They were introduced to us, and within seconds the tears started to flow. They cried. I cried. They were scared. I was scared. The gravity of the situation hit me. Their little souls had no idea what happened, and my mama heart broke for all their loss. For all their fear. I fully expected adoption to be challenging, but seeing fear in a two- and one-year-old's eyes broke my heart. I held each of them. I caressed their backs as I told them I loved them. They cried, screaming for the familiarity of the baby home.

Each of us holding a child wrapped in our arms, Derek and I looked into their bright brown eyes and told them how much we loved them. We gave our two-year-old the name Jericho, mentioned in the book of Joshua. It was a city within the Promised Land, an entrance to the heartland of Canaan. Jericho is listed as the first city Joshua and the Israelites conquered as they took the Promised Land. Jericho was a gift Israel had to fight for. The name seemed like a perfect fit.

We named our one-year-old Lucius. A source of light. A light that brings warmth and truth to dark places.

I took a deep breath as snot from Jericho dripped down my navy blue cotton dress. This is my life now: to begin to care for two traumatized babies. It was the first day of a nearly four-month stay in Uganda. We began to navigate the in-country guardianship process. Thousands of miles away from our community.

Love and Struggle

We can all easily trust God in the joyous seasons of life, but what about during the hard ones? Those are the times when we find who we really are. What we really believe. Those are the times when we grow our faith or we let it die. It is in our trials that our identity is tested. If we have poorly planted our seeds in the soil of security, safety, or good feelings, we will soon find out. We will find out if we truly believe God is sovereign. If we can believe His plan may include asking us to endure unthinkable acts, we will find out if our soul is settled in the death and resurrection of Jesus. Not a surname. Not an income. Not a family. We will find out if we really think we are image bearers, loved by God no matter what happens.

In rocky seasons, we may cling to God or blame God. Blame seems to make sense to us. Blame seems to give us answers to our burning questions. If we didn't get ourselves into the mess, then we will certainly nail the one who did. When we blame God, we feel validated—pointing out what we perceive to be His wrongdoings, His failures, and His shortcomings. We elevate ourselves to the throne of our hearts when we blame God. We take His seat and expect that if we just take control of our lives we can somehow sidestep the curve balls that are headed straight for us. We declare we don't need Him. We can do this on our own. The truth grows foggy, and we lose sight of what treasure could be found in the communion of dark moments. We blame God for all life's dreadful experiences.

Our anger is an emotion to be attended to. It is an emotion that is necessary to help us locate the source of our growing distress. Anger at God for our tender hurt is nothing new. It is also nothing God can't handle. He welcomes our honest emotions. He welcomes our rawest thoughts. We don't have to keep anger suppressed in the name of perfection. We can throw a punch at the sky. He can take it. Anger doesn't mean we have abandoned God; it means we have issues to work through. It means we need to know where He is in our troubles and if He is even present. Anger is valid and useful, but it is when we allow anger to spiral into blame then we have gotten ourselves in real trouble.

Something inside of us expects life to be perfect. We expect everything to bend our way. While I would be first in line for free cupcakes and world peace, I know that is not always my reality. My reality is that life is hard and suffering is imminent. It is because of the brokenness that surrounds me that Christ came for me. Christ is not the author of all atrocities; He is the Savior of all souls. We can take heart because He has overcome the world (John 16:33). The love of God and the struggle of humanity coexist. It isn't one or the other. Love and struggles are a package deal. God is not a traitor we can blame when we feel wronged. His is not a faulty love but a holy, unconditional love that stands with us.

Exhausted but Overjoyed

From the first day, caring for Jericho and Lucius left Derek and me exhausted. In our focused efforts to bond with two little ones, we fought off faithless feelings creeping in to our day—morning, noon, and night. From our guesthouse, we could hear the cries of other orphans in the night as we clutched our two precious boys in our arms. Everywhere we went, our eyes met faces of destitution and hunger. I had traveled to third-world countries for missions trips before, but never with the intent of inviting two children home with me. Two children who knew firsthand the effects of such loss. While surrounded by the suffering of so many orphans and witnessing the trauma of loss in my own two babies, a sadness crept into my once sturdy mind of peace. We were invited to be the parents of Jericho and Lucius as an answer to tragedy. I was certain that the Lord intended for this to build my faith, not to destroy it.

The smallest faith can make room for the great faithfulness of the Father.

Still, exhausted, impatient, and a little disheartened, we waited week after week for movement toward finalizing our guardianship, only to be met with unanticipated roadblocks that left us waiting still longer. During this time, we prayed for the intervention of God, for the next chapter of our story to begin. In the stillness, I fought off lies of God as unavailable, unreliable, and uninvolved in my present struggle. How wrong I was. By His very nature, God is steadfast. He is immovable. He is durable. He perseveres. The steadfast love of the Lord never ceases; his mercies never come to an end; they are new every morning; great is His faithfulness (Lamentations 3:22-23).

While our love for God may be fickle, the love from God does not fluctuate with our changing emotions. His love for us is not dependent on our love for Him. While we may find that we cannot count on much in this world, we can count on the love of God every single time. His love is the only thing that can outlast and withstand the tornados of torment that blow through our souls.

First Peter 1:7 says, "These trials will show that your faith is genuine. It is being tested as fire tests and purifies gold—though your faith is far more precious than mere gold. So when your faith remains strong through many trials, it will bring you much praise and glory and honor on the day when Jesus Christ is revealed to the whole world" (NLT). The very best way for faith to grow is through trials. It is belief, not blame, that will usher us into the kingdom of God, walking as daughters of light and truth.

Belief Against the Odds

The story of the woman who had an issue with blood, described in the Gospels (Matthew 9:20-22; Mark 5:25-34; Luke 8:43-48), is a beautiful example of what happens when we depend on Jesus for the outcome of our sorrowful situations. When we crave just a touch from Him, this account is a reminder that He won't ignore us when we push past worry to a place of belief. The truth is, when we reach out, groping in the dark, we'll find Jesus.

Luke 8:43-48 tells her story:

> A woman in the crowd had suffered for twelve years with constant bleeding, and she could find no cure. Coming up behind Jesus, she touched the fringe of his robe. Immediately, the bleeding stopped.
>
> "Who touched me?" Jesus asked.
>
> Everyone denied it, and Peter said, "Master, this whole crowd is pressing up against you."
>
> But Jesus said, "Someone deliberately touched me, for I felt healing power go out from me." When the woman realized that she could not stay hidden, she began to tremble and fell to her knees in front of him. The whole crowd heard her explain why she had touched him and that she had been immediately healed. "Daughter," he said to her, "your faith has made you well. Go in peace." (NLT)

This woman, who had bled for twelve years, was at the mercy of doctors who tried all their best practices to fix her. Broke and humiliated, she grew worse year after year. Can you imagine? No running water or modern sewer lines. She was ashamed, covered in her own blood, weak, considered untouchable, and an outcast from her family and her community. Perhaps she felt justified in her anger and resentment. Her life was seemingly against her, yet in her darkness, she chose the impossible: to believe. She chose to believe that Jesus was who He said He was. A Healer. A Savior. Here on earth, but about His heavenly Father's work.

In our waiting, He strengthens the foundations of our faith as the enemy of our hearts looks to weaken them.

She knew she had to fight to get to Him. She knew it wouldn't be easy. He was surrounded by people and she, bleeding out, would never be permitted an audience with Him. She was unclean. Broken. Damaged goods. Yet her faith, her belief that He could do something about her issue, was enough. Her trust in the power and sovereignty of Jesus made a way for her to believe that her life could get better. Her life could change. The smallest faith can make room for the great faithfulness of the Father. It can make room for the impossible. It can make room for the healing our hearts have always needed.

Jesus calls this dear woman with the issue of blood a daughter. This daughter, not of an absent father but of a faithful Father, is beloved and cherished. He indicates relationship. The power that left

Him when she touched the hem of His garment was transmitted to her because of her belief, her trust in the Godman.

First John 5:4-5 tells us, "Every child of God can defeat the world, and our faith is what gives us the victory. No one can defeat the world without having faith in Jesus as the Son of God" (CEV). Our faith in Jesus, even when battered and worn, will serve us well. It will not betray us. It may be the only thing that holds us together.

The woman with the issue of blood could have blamed God for her circumstance. She did not choose her condition. It chose her. When the opportunity came to encounter Jesus, she didn't scream, kick, or punch Him for her debilitating condition. She didn't wag a finger in His face. Instead, she believed. She believed He was capable of healing her failing body. Belief ushers in more hope than blame ever will. Blame leaves us restless and angry. It's a never-ending cycle of blame to assume God causes our pain.

Sarah Bessey, popular author, hit the nail on the head when she said:

> I couldn't trust God if I suspected God was behind our deepest grievances and injustices. This is where the sovereignty conversations get interesting, I know. But I don't blame God for much anymore. I see God as the rescue from the injustices, not the cause of them. I see God as the redeemer of the pain, not the origin of it. I see sovereignty, not as hyper-control over the minute and painful details of the world, but as a faithful promise that all things will be restored, all things will be redeemed, all will be rescued.[3]

Tested

Our faith is uniquely tested as we wait for a breakthrough. In waiting, we groan for the camaraderie of Jesus. We discover He is all we need. In anticipation of God's divine hand, we may feel the ground quake and slip out from under us, but Jesus alone is the lifter of our heads (Psalm 3:3). In our waiting, He strengthens the foundations of our faith as the enemy of our hearts looks to weaken them. We wait, in hopeful expectation, not with bitterness and resentment. As time passes, day after day, year after year, our hearts can grow weary wondering if Jesus will show up in our lives. A steadfast spirit gives us the grit to hold on while help is on the way, a breakthrough only Jesus can provide.

After sixty days in Uganda with little progress in our case, I feared the worst. I wondered if I'd return home barren. Would I go back home without sons to squeal in their nursery or fall asleep on my lap as I rocked them to sleep? The long wait left me with two options: worship or worry. In worship, we claim the God of All as our Advocate, our Comforter, our Deliverer. We believe He can do the impossible as He holds us tight. We are reminded that He is greater than anything inside or outside of us. We are reminded He can block the punches of the enemy, as He swings straight for our jaws. In worship, I'm led to fight for my faith and breakthrough in the life-saving power of Jesus. Allowing Him to do every ounce of heavy lifting.

First Peter 5:6-7 says, "Therefore humble yourselves under the mighty hand of God [set aside self-righteous pride], so that He may exalt you [to a place of honor in His service] at the appropriate time, casting all your cares [all your anxieties, all your worries, and all your concerns, once and for all] on Him, for He cares about you [with deepest affection, and watches over you very carefully]" (AMP).

At the right time, Jesus will, as we have trusted and believed in His very nature, do what we thought impossible. He is an on-time Provider. No mistakes. No missteps. If we allow it to be, our waiting can be beautiful, full of opportunities to bolster our belief in His glorious nature. When He does make a move, it will celebrate the faith that was already present in our lives, even if it's only the size of a mustard seed. He leaves us speechless over His mercy and providence. It's nothing we can conjure up on our own.

While I didn't get what I wanted in those first sixty days in Uganda, I am glad I didn't know there would be nearly sixty more. Despair would have gotten the best of me. Instead, I found myself daily muttering, shouting, and sobbing prayers of belief. I was pregnant with the promise of sons. My own heart and the world around me was served best by my growing faith, not by my debilitating dread. The days of waiting were a faith builder.

As Philippians 4:6-7 says so well, "Do not be anxious or worried about anything, but in everything [every circumstance and situation] by prayer and petition with thanksgiving, continue to make your [specific] requests known to God. And the peace of God [that peace which reassures the heart, that peace] which transcends all understanding, [that peace which] stands guard over your hearts and your minds in Christ Jesus [is yours]" (AMP).

Not from a prosperous position but a dark dungeon, Paul penned the book of Philippians. He was no stranger to bleak situations as he encouraged the early church, and us, to pray through our heartache for our own allowances of peace.

Peace is ours even in the midst of turmoil. Even in the midst of waiting. Even in the midst of what feels like faltering faith. His peace stands guard over our hearts. Peace guides us through the maze of worry. It's the gift in the waiting. We may not have the answers to our problems, but peace harkens us to the heart of God. His peace will sustain us in the trying moments of cancer treatments, failing marriages, job losses, or stalled adoptions. We can exchange our blame for belief, our worry for peace. This is life hidden in Christ. It is a never-ending communion that can withstand the gloomiest of days.

John 14:27 says that Jesus offers those who follow Him a treasured possession, "Peace I leave with you; my peace I give you. I do not give to you as the world gives. Do not let your hearts be troubled and do not be afraid." It's the very peace that sustained Jesus throughout His time on earth that's available to us.

In his commentary, *The Great Texts of the Bible*, James Hastings elaborates on the peace of Jesus:

> Jesus defines the peace which He was leaving to the disciples as that peace which He had Himself enjoyed: "My peace I give unto you,"—as one hands over a possession he has himself tested, the shield or helmet that has served him in battle. "That which has protected Me in a thousand fights I make over to you." The peace which Christ desires His disciples to enjoy is that which characterized Himself; the same serenity in danger, the same equanimity in troublous circumstances, the same freedom from anxiety about results, the same speedy recovery of composure after something had for a moment ruffled the calm surface of His demeanour. This is what He makes over to His people; this is what He makes possible to all who serve Him.[4]

Christ gives us the same peace that He Himself enjoyed by leading us to the throne room of God. A place where we are not shamed by a loveless God, rather where we are redeemed by a Benevolent One. A place where we find ourselves becoming more of who we were always meant to be, for we are not of this world but within it.

With the Giver, we can be at peace. At peace with ourselves. At peace with others. As Hastings says of peace, "our antidote to all dismay and despondency." That's our Jesus. That's our King. No matter what tests our faith, He can be the anchor, heavy with peace, to secure our soul.

CHAPTER NINE

Bitterness

I tend to lean toward optimism. I can't help but hope for the best because I'm terrified of things going wrong. Maybe it's my way of shedding the coat of worry. But things do go wrong. More often than I'd like. When life doesn't bend my way, I do have options. I can get bitter or I can . . . oh, wait, what are my other options? Bitterness, like a Carolina tick, burrows its head in deep. It's after the unseen. That's where it does its best work. It takes the life right out of me. It's not flashy like anger or pouty like jealousy. It goes deep and rewires how I see others. How I see God. Bitterness may often be my first response to frustrating times, but I don't want it to be my last.

Bitterness isn't a stranger to any of us. It is obnoxious and unhelpful, but it sure seems to know our business. It is sometimes felt with its best buddies: anger and vengeance. Still, even as a solo act it can do serious damage to our souls. Bitterness separates us from the grace of God. It's a slick sin that we slip into and we justify it in rocky times as our only foothold.

When we have a bitter heart, we feel justified in our feelings. We withhold grace from those who have wronged us. We may even describe bitterness as protection. It's not. Bitterness is beating us up, bruising our hearts. From the inside out.

Bitterness is a root issue in our lives. Over time it will likely sprout into anger. An anger that turns into ever-increasing demands of God and others. Our bitterness causes expectations that the Father and those around us will fix our problems and will give us the apologies we think we deserve. If demands aren't met we continue to wallow in bitterness, in our hearts and often in our words.

Bitterness is dangerous. It is poisonous to the well of our hearts and the wells of others. It contaminates our thoughts until we lose sight of what we wanted in the first place. A harmonious life with Christ. Bitterness isn't the only possible outcome of the times that incite it in us. There is an option far sweeter, neither just bitter nor just sweet. Instead, there is bittersweet; the two meld together to give us a taste of both the tragic and magic in life.

Everything, both past and present, calls out for a Savior.

Shauna Niequist describes it beautifully in her book, *Bittersweet*:

> The idea of bittersweet is changing the way I live, unraveling and re-weaving the way I understand life. Bittersweet is the idea that in all things there is both something broken and something beautiful, that there is a sliver of lightness on even the darkest of nights, a shadow of hope in every heartbreak, and that rejoicing is no less rich when it contains a splinter of sadness.
>
> Bittersweet is the practice of believing that we really do need both the bitter and the sweet, and that a life of nothing but sweetness rots both your teeth and the soul. Bitter is what makes us strong, what forces us to push through, what helps us earn the lines on our faces and the calluses on our hands. Sweet is nice enough, but bitterness is beautiful, nuanced, full of depth and complexity. Bittersweet is courageous, gutsy, earthy.[1]

It's the understanding that life is bittersweet that staves off bitter memories and thoughts. This understanding helps us find light in the most unlikely places, people, and past seasons.

All My Nevers

We were still in Uganda. It had been seventy days. Our skins were marked with sharp tan lines and our hearts were marked with love for two children who called us Mama and Dada. All four of us had settled into our new roles. Each morning we'd start the day around 7:00 a.m. with snuggles and books. Derek and I ate our breakfast of toast, eggs, and banana, each of us with a child on our lap. After breakfast, we'd clean up the splash zone and pull out the few toys we had brought with us. Two board books, two soft footballs, and empty water bottles were placed on the concrete floor for the boys to play with while I sipped my hot coffee. Mornings turned to afternoons, and the warm sun would grow blazing hot. We would make a game of washing our clothes and hanging them out to dry. Any chore helped pass the time. Once lunch was finished, we'd lay our sons down to nap. With two hours to ourselves, we would write, study, or pass the time with as much laughter as we could conjure up in our time of waiting. Finally, we were only seven days away from our anticipated court date and our hopes were high. The end was surely in sight. With big prayers, we imagined we'd be heading home sooner than later.

Then a knock on the door changed everything.

It was 3:00 p.m. The boys perked up when they heard the knuckles hit the door of our bedroom. I opened it to find out we were being summoned to discuss our impending court case. I bounced down the stairs and met our legal counsel with smiles. He met me with solemn eyes and clenched lips. In English, he explained that we would no longer be able to pursue guardianship of Lucius. I misunderstood him at first. I asked him to tell me again. He repeated his news, and like a knife to the heart, my heart fell into two pieces. Derek stared at me with fright-filled eyes. We held each other. We wept. We didn't even wait until we returned to our room. We couldn't have, even if we had tried. Our dream of raising Lucius, of holding him tight, and of our sweet family of four was dead. Never to be revived.

There was nothing we could do.

I could see before me all the nevers. Lucius would never nap in his nursery prepared at home. He'd never wear the winter onesies meant for him, gifts from my baby shower. He'd never sit in the double stroller with his brother as we walked around the neighborhood. My dreams of celebrating birthday parties, Christmas mornings, swimming lessons, first crushes, teaching him to drive, family vacations, high school graduation, choosing colleges, his wedding, and my grandbabies were gone in an instant. I had no idea what would happen to him. The seventy days of consistency we had managed to develop and the little gains we had made had come to a screeching halt. His precious smile and jovial personality would now be only in my memories, not in my future.

Without many solid answers to our multiple questions, we chose to worship the Lord out of gratitude and desperation. We were grateful the Lord had led us to a place of ultimate trust in Him but desperate for Him to show us His loving hand in our circumstances. So we worshiped until we felt His peace—silently worshiping through our court dates and interviews at the US Embassy and worshiping together during the long nights when we thought we might leave Uganda barren. The Lord had prompted us to worship through both the low moments *and* the high moments. We discovered firsthand that it is worship that keeps our hearts set on the plans of God rather than our own.

We had seven more days together as a family of four. We spent every waking moment whispering teary prayers over a baby we'd never see again. We cuddled, cooed, and sang. We savored every laugh, giggle, and smile that our little light gave us. We took video after video, snapped photo after photo. I wanted to remember every sound, every smile, every cuddle. Even though we'd been in Uganda for what felt like forever, I suddenly found myself begging time to stand still. I wanted every single minute to last for hours, to last forever.

When we said our good-byes, it was one of the toughest moments of my life. Joy and connection were stolen. It was my own dark night of the soul. When they took him from us, I secretly hoped he would transition with little tears, but like a nightmare he screamed and wailed as he reached for us. We couldn't reach back. He was gone forever.

Bittersweet

In our deep lament, our heaviness is more than the human heart can bear. This was never the original plan. It wasn't the plan to endure unthinkable tragedy that would leave our hearts aching and broken. When our first mother and father left the garden, weapons of destruction pierced all of our hearts in the shape of a sharp grief that we carry like stones. Throughout generations all of humanity have faced insurmountable obstacles that wreak havoc on our souls. Life gives us bitter moments. But in the bitter we can find the sweet if we look for it.

We can spot its existence from the very beginning:

Now the LORD God had planted a garden in the east, in Eden; and there he put the man he had formed. The LORD God made all

kinds of trees grow out of the ground—trees that were pleasing
to the eye and good for food. In the middle of the garden were
the tree of life and the tree of the knowledge of good and evil.
(Genesis 2:8-9)

The LORD God took the man and put him in the Garden of Eden
to work it and take care of it. And the LORD God commanded
the man, "You are free to eat from any tree in the garden; but you
must not eat from the tree of the knowledge of good and evil, for
when you eat from it you will certainly die." (Genesis 2:15-17)

Now the serpent was more crafty than any of the wild animals
the LORD God had made. He said to the woman, "Did God really
say, 'You must not eat from any tree in the garden'?"

The woman said to the serpent, "We may eat fruit from the
trees in the garden, but God did say, 'You must not eat fruit from
the tree that is in the middle of the garden, and you must not
touch it, or you will die.'"

"You will not certainly die," the serpent said to the woman.
"For God knows that when you eat from it your eyes will be
opened, and you will be like God, knowing good and evil."

When the woman saw that the fruit of the tree was good for
food and pleasing to the eye, and also desirable for gaining wisdom, she took some and ate it. She also gave some to her husband, who was with her, and he ate it. Then the eyes of both of
them were opened, and they realized they were naked; so they
sewed fig leaves together and made coverings for themselves.

Then the man and his wife heard the sound of the LORD God
as he was walking in the garden in the cool of the day, and they
hid from the LORD God among the trees of the garden. (Genesis
3:1-8)

After their encounter with Father God, the man and woman were banished from Eden forever. Never to return. Death entered the world and sin was born because of their choices. It seemed that nothing good could come out of that disobedience, but there was a silver lining. In that bitter moment, sweet was on its way. All of Scripture points to the universal need for a Savior, someone greater, someone better, someone true for our physical, mental, emotional, communal, political, and societal needs.

Everything, both past and present, calls out for a Savior. Writer Raechel Myers, says of Adam, "While the whole of the Old Testament world groaned under the weight of its own imperfection—unfaithful, unbelieving, and incomplete—we, the Church, now see with clearer eyes that 'all the promises of God find their "Yes" in Christ' (2 Corinthians 1:20). The world would always be incomplete without Jesus."[2]

The bitter in Adam's story led to the sweet for us all—grace found in Jesus, new life, and no sting in death. Sin and death entered the world through Adam by one act. Everyone dies because everyone sins (Romans 5:17). Life-giving reparation was given by Jesus through one truly righteous act because He was the One righteous man (Romans 5:18).

If Jesus can bring sweet redemption, grace, and hope to Adam's situation, He will certainly offer honey to sweeten our bitter times. Bitter times are inevitable, but to embrace bitterness is a choice. No matter what's happened to us we can ask the Good Father to give us honey, to help us find sweet treasures to assuage the heaviness. No matter if it is our own sin for which we repent and ask for grace, or for the sins of others who have hurt us. Either offer His presence. Either can produce for us precious gems of sweetness.

If we aren't able to identify our bitter times as possibly sweet, we'll miss any opportunity available to encounter Christ or any good gift He is offering to us. I think there are a few things at play here: we live in the natural world; and when something bad happens, our human tendency is to move on, shrink back, or remove ourselves as quickly as we can from the situation. We separate everything. What's bitter is bitter and what's sweet is sweet.

Sometimes we miss the sweetening in our stories when we harbor disbelief. We find it unimaginable that God would offer us something good because of our own bad choices. We feel shame for who we are and what we have done. The enemy does his best work in the lying labyrinth of shame. As we have already established, he isolates us with twisted lies and defeating thoughts. If we're drinking from the fire hose of shame we'll never identify the sweet treasure that is ours to taste. We disqualify ourselves from any healing if we're overcome with shame. We believe that sweet moments and sweet gifts are for everyone else sitting around us and not us. They *are* for us.

Other times we wallow in bitterness because we don't understand how God can allow tragedy. I have a friend who is going through something tough. She said to me, "I don't feel like a beloved child of God in this. How could this be my life when I've listened to Him?"

When I offered my answer about God's love for her, she responded with, "Well, then why is this happening?" Perhaps she forgot that our faith in Jesus does not disqualify us from troubles. No matter what season we are in, God is a giver of good things. He isn't a distant father who visits twice a year. He hasn't abandoned us. If we find ourselves questioning God's goodness to us we need to take a step back. Breathe deep and remember we are beloved. That's nonnegotiable. It's not on the table for discussion.

We can't always control what happens to us, but we can always control how we choose to respond. When we get angry and push God away, He waits until we're ready. He's a gentleman. Without Him we'll crumble under the weight of our circumstances. If our lives are deeply rooted in Christ and our character is daily being shaped by His Holy Spirit, then we'll respond differently. It's understandable to run to God in our tragedy, but to run to Him daily, regardless of how we feel, is the difference maker. He longs for daily communion with us more than us knowing Him at rock bottom. First Thessalonians 5:16-18 offers us encouragement for our growing faith, "Rejoice always, pray continually, give thanks in all circumstances; for this is God's will for you in Christ Jesus."

The Father is a Comforter. He wipes our tears, holds us tight, and reveals the sweet, silver lining of our bitter times, Himself.

We still crave the lush Garden of Eden. Adam was surrounded by everything literally and figuratively sweet in the garden. When he was banished, he, Eve, and all humanity to come would forever find themselves seeking what was lost. We have hunted for Eden's luxury and safety in all the wrong places. We have tapped the hearts of parents, friends, boyfriends, husbands, pastors, and mentors, looking for just a drop of honey. While we have found goodness in others, that goodness does not replace what we have lost. Some of us look for the sweet in a pill, a bottle, a body, or any other distraction that can overwhelm our senses. It is our search for Eden. It is our search for a perfect place. A place of no pain, no loss, no sin. A place where we are bare before our Creator. A place where we are loved, cherished, valued, respected, and fulfilled.

The decision to be bitter or to grasp the sweet will lead us to a desert or an oasis of the soul. Or we can have them both. When we embrace sweet treasures in bitter times, we understand the world, that folly does not surpass God's love and passion for us. Every promise of God finds its yes in Jesus. In that moment, when we choose to accept the bittersweet, we are rebuilt because we are with Him. He is present in the bittersweet. He will redeem us. He will save us. He will make His home in us. Nothing will be left behind in His pursuit of us, to restore and reclaim all that's been lost.

In Sara Hagerty's book, *Every Bitter Thing Is Sweet*, she writes, "I don't want to be a hungry soul just for a season. I want to live hunger. This is what draws me to Him. This is what fills every single bitter circumstance with the opportunity to know Him more. This is what brings me to the sweetness of His presence. And hope happens here at this nexus of bitter and sweet."[3]

If we choose to embrace even the smallest shred of sweet in bitter times we will find a comfort we had no idea was possible this side of heaven. We will discover the comfort of Christ. Second Corinthians 1:3-4 tells us, "Blessed be the God and Father of our Lord Jesus Christ, the Father of mercies and God of all comfort, who comforts us in all our affliction, so that we may be able to comfort those who are in any affliction, with the comfort with which we ourselves are comforted by God" (ESV).

Strong's *Concordance* clarifies that the words *all comfort* come from the ancient Greek word *paraklesis*.[4] What this word implies is more than a pacifying sympathy. It suggests strength, help, and bravery. We are made stronger by the God of all comfort. God is a holy

God capable of giving us Himself: comfort, strength, bravery, and courage.

My Comforter met me as I poured out my grief at losing Lucius. I sat with a grief counselor and explained the bitter biting moment. She listened and heard every word I uttered, describing his drooly smile, his soft skin, and how he wobbled as he learned to walk. I explained my deep belief that Lucius's heart knew he was loved and cherished. I feared the worst for his life but hoped for the best. I apologized for the ugly display of emotion as I cried uncontrollably, wiping my tears on the sleeves of my sweater.

My counselor asked if she could pray with me and if we could invite Jesus into my bitter moment. She asked if Jesus would make Himself plain on that dark day. She asked if He would comfort me. My weeping fell to silence as I sensed the good and comforting presence of Jesus that had been there in the very moment that my precious Lucius left my arms. It was an intervention of His comfort. It was His warmth. I was not alone on the day I gave my sweet baby away. Jesus was with me. I was never alone. It was unlike anything I had ever experienced before. My story was rewritten.

As we seek to heal and we walk into the fullness of God ahead of us, we can allow Him to help us see our past with Him in it. He revises our reflections. He gives us eyes to see Himself weaved in and through our painful narrative. The Father is a Comforter. He wipes our tears, holds us tight, and reveals the sweet, silver lining of our bitter times, Himself.

Birthday Cake and Bitter Herbs

A couple of years ago at Bible study, my group worked our way through a few bittersweet moments found in Scripture. We talked about reclaiming what has been lost or taken, about claiming the bittersweet: the comfort in bitter moments in Jesus and others and lastly, that day, in the shadow of Easter. We talked about Christ's sacrifice and His gift to us of the ultimate "sweet" in our bitter times.

One night in particular, I was brought to tears when a dear friend brought a birthday cake to Bible study after reading my blog in which I had written of the struggle to celebrate Lucius's birthday. We sang the birthday song and prayed over his life, for his health, and for the Lord to be near to him, to hold him, and to keep him. It had been three years since I had seen Lucius. My celebration of God's past faithfulness through a bitter season proved to be a mirror of what our hearts discovered over the course of the evening's Bible study.

"There is no fellowship of His glory without the fellowship of His suffering."

We studied the Passover and its significance. We highlighted the symbolism of the bitter herbs, which reminded Israel of their enslavement in Egypt, of their suffering and pain at the hands of Pharaoh, and of their sin and need for a Savior. Then the matzah, the unleavened bread that represented a sinless life to be sacrificed.

The Passover reminded us that the bitter and the sweet often arrive hand in hand. John 16:33 reminds us, "In this world you will have trouble. But take heart! I have overcome the world."

As the night progressed, we discussed the four cups of wine served at Passover:

The Cup of Sanctification. It symbolized Israel's deliverance from being under the burdens of the Egyptians.

The Cup of Deliverance. It symbolized Israel's deliverance from their bondage.

The Cup of Redemption. It symbolized God's promise to redeem Israel with an outstretched arm.

The Cup of Praise. It symbolized the fact that God took the Israelites to be His people.

As we studied each of these, another friend shared what Jesus revealed through her own sanctification, deliverance, redemption, and praise. She opened her testimony with a timely truth, sharing, "There is no fellowship of His glory without the fellowship of His suffering."

If we seek to know His praise, to know His nature, there must be a reason why. There must be something that drives us to the place of knowing and seeking His face. In our bitter days, He will be our Comfort, our Deliverer from burdens and bondage. He will be our Redeemer and He will be our Father. Our bitter times can be the sweetest seasons of our lives.

As that night drew to a close I couldn't help but think of what we all have lost in the garden (His presence and companionship) we can all claim in the desert. It is our promise. In Exodus 16:1-36, we find insight into God's deliverance for the people of Israel in a passage that has no shortage on complaining or wondering if God was near and one particular verse sticks out to me as I think of desert moments. It is verse 10: "While Aaron was speaking to the whole Israelite community, they looked toward the desert, and there was the glory of the LORD appearing in the cloud."

His presence, the glory of the LORD in a cloud, was found in the desert, available to heal, restore, redeem, and deliver. This is who He is. No matter which winds knock you flat on your face, He is for you, near in your bitter times, and His promises are yours to claim. His promise of comfort is yours. His promise of deliverance is yours. His promise of redemption is yours. His promise to be your Father is always yours. He will not forsake you. He will not leave you.

He won't waste your bitter moments. He'll sneak in the sweetness your soul needs to sustain it through the unthinkable. When you let go of shame, when you remember God is good no matter what, and when you rely on your faith, you will most certainly find His treasures in darkness (Isaiah 45:3). Like honey in the mouth of a lion's carcass (Judges 14:8). Bitterness will gladly take up space in your soul but we must opt to choose the better thing, we must embrace the bittersweet.

CHAPTER TEN

Hopelessness

We find ourselves at the impasse of hopelessness when we believe our situation is outside the realm of God's sovereign hand. We throw up our questions and hear no answers. When we have a hopeless heart, disappointment pulls us down and sinks the foundation of our beliefs, our hope. Jesus, the Author and Finisher of our faith.

We may have arrived at hopelessness, not by God's bidding but by our own. He is not handing out disappointment. He is not looking to rough us up in the name of righteousness. He is a sovereign God who offers hope to our tender souls. Jesus is not the thief of hope. He is the Giver of hope.

Rock Bottom

The day before our heartrending good-bye to Lucius we made our way to the high court in the center of Kampala, Uganda. Gussied up in our Sunday best, we sat in a crowded courtroom hoping to pursue guardianship of Jericho. I listened as best I could to the native language, Luganda, spit back and forth between the judge, lawyers, and witnesses. From tense faces and stone-cold body language, I quickly discerned that the odds were not leaning toward our favor. My heart raced and sweat dripped down my back as we waited for the verdict. After hours in a packed courtroom, our case was deemed "inconclusive." It was not a no. It was not a yes. On paper, I was not yet his mother, but there was still a chance I would be.

Deflated and worn out, I dragged myself down three flights of stairs to get back in to our van. Aboard the van with Derek and the other witnesses to our case, I clutched Jericho on my lap and stroked his back as he dozed off to sleep. I couldn't eat. I couldn't drink. I could hardly speak. I just wanted it to be over. I just wanted to go home with my son. In that somber moment, I feared I'd go home alone.

As we sat in the bumper-to-bumper traffic on the journey back to our guesthouse, I questioned the story God was writing. Was I going home barren? Was I going back home, not with two children, nor one child, but rather dead-of-the-winter barren? It sure felt like it. I didn't see how things could bend our way. I didn't see the light at the end of my never-ending twisty, turning tunnel. I wondered if there even was a light to begin with. Was this some sick cosmic joke on my tender desire to be a mother? Why had this all happened? I couldn't take another day of it. It was too hard. My faith cracked under the weight of the struggle. I was barely hanging on.

If we are to hope in Jesus Christ, we must lend ourselves to circumstances outside our control as we dance to the rhythm of obedience.

With a gargantuan thud, I had hit rock bottom. I was hopeless. Most of the time during the lengthy adoption process I had managed to keep my hopes high. I was solid in my beliefs. Without a doubt, two brown-eyed boys were going to be my sons. I was certain, until that day. Knowing we would say good-bye to Lucius in one day's time after that discouraging court date, I had no gumption left. My soul strained under the heartache.

With Jericho's sweaty, sleeping body across my lap, I reminisced about my baby shower the year before. A dear friend, Lisa, led a devotional time and shared about the Israelite's famous march around Jericho. Full of hope, the people of God claimed the gift their Father had given them. It was a promise, and they actively pursued it. Toward the end of her message, Lisa explained that when they took the walled city, the warriors went first with swords drawn, the priests went second with praises lifted high to the King, and the ark of the covenant went last. She instructed me that my children will go before me, I will pray with the priesthood, and the presence of the Lord will be there for it all. At the climax of her message she pulled a sword from its sheath and asked Derek and I to hold it, with belief in the promise of our son, as she led us in a fiery prayer. It was a powerful moment I treasured.

Now, hopeless and distraught, I slumped in that steamy bus and wondered if the Lord remembered our passionate prayers for Jericho. Maybe my hope and prayers weren't enough? I wondered if he was present, like the ark of the covenant, for the people of God. If He was with them, would He be with me?

Rhythm of Obedience

For a believing woman, it baffles me to no end when I am obedient to the will of God and I don't see the outcomes I expect. When I held tight to His vision but came up empty-handed. Not rewarded for obedience but instead left with tears and ashes. It doesn't make a lick of sense. The high-stakes journey of following after Jesus is this: we aren't responsible for the outcomes, only for the obedience. As good, obedient lovers of Jesus, who listen to the whispers of the Holy Spirit, we are not exempt from tragedy or distress when we are in the wild will of the Father. We will have bad days. We may be willfully sailing into rough waters when we choose the ways of God.

We navigate the choppy waves full of hope that God will calm the waters. We believe that He will show up in our time of need, especially if He is the one who talked us into venturing onto that boat in the first place. In our belief, we learn about the true nature of hope—what it is and what it isn't.

---

*Our influence, gains, and losses pale
in comparison to the all-surpassing
knowledge of life with Christ.*

Hope isn't in ourselves. We are strong women, and we have literal and figurative scars to prove it. However, if we get caught up in overconfidence we may miss the mark of holding fast to our True Hope. We'll cut Jesus right out of the picture. We'll hope in our own strength. We will forget our finite and fallible backbones. The honest truth is that we can't do it all and be it all. We weren't even meant to live that way. Each of us is a masterpiece. Escorted through life by the Hope Giver. If we carry on living in a mere sliver of the life He intended for us, we can certainly hope in ourselves; we can believe we are the masters of our destiny. If we are to hope in Jesus Christ, we must lend ourselves to circumstances outside our control as we dance to the rhythm of obedience. We may just two-step ourselves right in situations in which we need a miracle and that's OK. To avoid risk is to avoid the space where miracles happen.

When we place hope in our wavering situations, we hope in the unsettling outward and not the certain inward. We hope in the changing versus the unchangeable. It's a poor investment to hope in our circumstance, even if it's one to which we believe the Good Lord led us. He never leads us to hope or believe in anyone but Himself. Regardless of our financial situations, employment, social status, or church membership, our hope can be rooted in Jesus, not our standing. We are not meant to hope in our situations, but rather our situations are meant to drive us to hope in the Hope Giver—Jesus. If we bank on our situation all it takes is one wrong move or one unforeseen surprise and our house of cards will come crashing down. We will be left empty and disappointed.

Hold Fast

Lucius was gone whilst still in the midst of the adoption process for Jericho. With a fresh investigation underway, I steadied my tired hands and weak knees for whatever our new findings revealed. Without hesitation, Derek and I honored the judge's wishes and trusted that the Lord knew best for Jericho. Even if the outcome wasn't what we wanted. This wasn't about us. This was about a son without a family. Even if he didn't join our family I trusted the Lord would protect and care for him. Jericho belonged first and foremost to the Lord, who had his best interest at heart.

I remember writing a letter to a friend back home, stating, "I've found it foolish to put stock in my role as a mother, wife, or friend. I'm simply a believer. My hope is in Christ. It seems everything else is slipping away and Jesus has become my only Hope."

Our influence, gains, and losses pale in comparison to the all-surpassing knowledge of life with Christ. Paul says in Philippians 3:8

(NLT), "Yes, everything else is worthless when compared with the infinite value of knowing Christ Jesus my Lord. For his sake I have discarded everything else, counting it all as garbage, so that I could gain Christ" (NLT).

As we hope in Christ, He gives us guidance through our trials. My hope in Jesus blossomed in troublesome times, and it gave me a resolve to keep going. A hopeless heart wants to throw in the towel, but a hopeful one carries on. There are a million reasons to quit life, but hope gives a shoulder to lean on. It will carry us when we want nothing more than to sit down on the sidewalk and quit the race set before us.

Isaiah 40:31 reminds us:

> But those who hope in the LORD
> will renew their strength.
> They will soar on wings like eagles;
> they will run and not grow weary,
> they will walk and not be faint.

True hope says I trust in the power of God. I trust in the will of God. I trust in the way of God. I trust in the timing of God. Hope is not an emotion. It's a belief in the One who arranged the stars, knitted us together in our mother's womb, and knows us by name. It's a belief that we're loved, not rejected, by a good and holy God.

Nowhere in Scripture are we promised a trouble-free life if we follow Jesus. Too many of us are convinced that the Lord's primary objective is to make us happy. His primary objective is to make us holy by offering us a constant communion with Him. When we meditate on the promises of God, let us resolve to believe they do not exist to make our life easy, but instead they serve as aids to help us grow closer to Him.

Hebrews 10:19-23 instructs us:

> Therefore, brothers and sisters, since we have confidence to enter
> the Most Holy Place by the blood of Jesus, by a new and living
> way opened for us through the curtain, that is, his body, and since
> we have a great priest over the house of God, let us draw near to
> God with a sincere heart and with the full assurance that faith
> brings, having our hearts sprinkled to cleanse us from a guilty
> conscience and having our bodies washed with pure water. Let
> us hold unswervingly to the hope we profess, for he who prom-
> ised is faithful.

Hebrews was written to Jewish and Gentile believers, the chosen
people of God and the folks who were grafted into the story of salvation. Both parties had hope: a desire for something good and great
expectations. Ancient letters make up the book of Hebrews and serve
as an encouragement to persevere through persecution. Doubt had
settled in among the followers of Jesus. Disappointment was at an
all-time high in their lives as oppression left them destitute and tired.
Both the Jewish and Gentile believers, in their grief-stricken state,
questioned whether Jesus truly was the Savior. Their persecution was
an unwelcome affliction. They assumed they would live victorious
lives after He gave His own.

---

*None of us are disqualified from adversity
because of our faith in Jesus.*

Hebrews 10 reminds the early believers of the new covenant. They
have access to God because of the death and resurrection of Jesus.
The veil that separated the presence of the Lord from the people was

torn in two. They can abide in the power, love, and companionship of God through His Son. That offer did not exist until Jesus died for the sins of humanity. Under the new covenant, which we live by today, believers can approach the throne of God with boldness anytime they desire. Their communion with God is not subject to the law. They are not separated in any way from the powerful Creator of the world. They assumed such privilege would disqualify them from hardship, but they were gravely mistaken.

None of us are disqualified from adversity because of our faith in Jesus. We serve a King not of this world. He is not a king with a militant army that will guard us by gunfire. He is a holy high Priest, the Prophet of all prophets, a majestic King who is far more interested in advancing His kingdom through the unseen, the unchangeable. Worship, not warfare, will lead us to place our hope in Jesus. Hebrews 10 explains that hope will sustain us through hardship. It is hope, grown in the full assurance of faith, that will lead us through hell or high water. Not around it. Not over it. But through it.

We can hold unswervingly to our hope when our hope is placed deep in Jesus. Our hope is rooted in everything He is and stands for. Our hope is a person. Our hope is Jesus. Hebrews 10:23 reads, "Let us hold fast the confession of our hope without wavering, for he who promised is faithful" (ESV). We can only hold so fast or tight to something that is already holding fast to us. This means that Jesus has a grip on us, and it is not a grip that suffocates but a grip that sustains. Disappointment, as a result of hopelessness, is not rooted in Jesus. It is rooted in ourselves. Only when we hope in Jesus can we be free from the drowning waters of hopelessness. We are free from the false mastery of our imperfect selves and free from our ever-changing situations. These are but a counterfeit hope when it comes to Jesus.

Hebrews 6:19 adds to the imagery of hope when it says, "We have this hope as an anchor for the soul, firm and secure."

Matthew Henry expounds on Hebrews 6 when he says,

> The consolations of God are strong enough to support his people under their heaviest trials. Here is a refuge for all sinners who flee to the mercy of God, through the redemption of Christ, according to the covenant of grace, laying aside all other confidences. We are in this world as a ship at sea, tossed up and down, and in danger of being cast away. We need an anchor to keep us sure and steady. Gospel hope is our anchor in the storms of this world. It is sure and steadfast, or it could not keep us so. The free grace of God, the merits and mediation of Christ, and the powerful influences of his Spirit, are the grounds of this hope, and so it is a steadfast hope.[1]

> No sailor would take an ocean voyage in a ship without an anchor, because they understand that situations might arise when the "hope" of the ship will depend not so much on the captain but on the integrity of the anchor. When all people and systems fail, there remains a steadfast hope in the anchor.[2]

The Honest Truth

When we find ourselves stuck and slapping away hopeless feelings like a pesky gnat, we can remember our hope is not in our ability to believe the best in ourselves. It is not up to us. Hope is not found in our charm, wit, net worth, social standing, or connections. It is not found in the people we surround ourselves with. If we place counterfeit hope—a knock-off of the real thing—in people, we will end up disappointed. They are all as frail as you and me. They are not capable of the divine intervention that hope in Christ offers.

We don't have to sulk; our soul need not be disturbed and distressed. We can put our hope in God. We can praise Him. Our Savior and our God (Psalm 42:5). May we be strong and take heart, all who hope in the Lord (Psalm 31:24). If we hope in the Lord, we'll renew our strength. We will soar on wings like eagles; we will run and not grow weary, we will walk and not be faint (Isaiah 40:31).

David Murray, Professor of Theology at Puritan Reformed Theological Seminary, explains the virtues of hope:

- Hope moves us forward.
- Hope energizes the present.
- Hope lightens our darkness.
- Hope increases faith.
- Hope is infectious.
- Hope is practical.[3]

It is an unwavering hope in Jesus that can withstand the storms and reveal the good and perfect rescue of the Father. Our hopelessness will leave us disappointed, but our hope in Christ will unveil the power and sovereignty of God in our everyday life. Our catastrophes are no match for a deep, abiding hope in Jesus.

Circling the Promise of Jericho

On June 5, 2013, I had a particularly heavy heart. Our lawyer went back to court to present the findings of our final investigation. I waited, something I was exceedingly familiar with by that point. I hoped, cried, and called out to God to have His way. I asked Him to be my Hope no matter the outcome. At that very moment, as I sat on the couch, my teary prayers sprinkling the cup of green tea clutched to my chest, I received an e-mail. It was from a dear friend who explained that she felt prompted to get out of bed (it was about 2:00 a.m. on the West Coast) to pray for Jericho's case. On the other side of the world she was awake and feeling that it was a crucial hour and that she had been assigned to pray for God's good and perfect will. She made it clear she would not stop until she sensed the peace to do so. It was in the middle of the night for her and she had no idea our lawyer was in court that very moment. She continued to pray and check in every thirty minutes or so. After three hours, we got a message from our lawyer. It read, "It is done."

Hope stares in the eyes of the enemy and shouts of the eternal reward the Father offers through his Son.

Every anxious thought melted into a puddle at my feet as I knew exactly what the message implied.

It's done. It's done and I don't have to hope and wonder if I will be his mama. It's done and the judge has ruled that I, and my husband, will be his guardians. It's done and God has heard my cries. It's done and I have seen this very day the sovereign power of the Lord. I raced back to my computer to tell my friend, but instead I found a message from my dear prayer warrior that said, "It's over, isn't it? I'm going back to bed."

My Hope, my Jesus, ordered every moment according to His perfect plan. It was Christ's plan for me to circle my promise of adopting a son, trusting in the Lord for the victory. It was His plan that Jericho would join Derek and me to be a family even when it felt like all hope was lost. It was His plan that we would lean not on our own understanding or strength but in our weakness would declare He is strong. The Good Lord was *still* working out His plan when my plans fell apart.

Dark days will find us. They creep up when we least expect them. They choke us up, punch us in the gut, or leave us disappointed. Our belief in the One who can deliver us from tender hurts and heartache is dulled by disappointment. We must remember, in the dark, we do have a way forward. That way is hope. A hope that is untouchable and unsinkable.

Our hope is not found in our husbands, our parents, our children, our closest friends, our ego, our passions, our jobs, or our 401(k). So often, we misdirect our beliefs and affections to those people around us, most of whom are grasping for hope just as we are.

Hope says, "I am built for life in Christ. I won't be worn down by my circumstance but held in the palm of the Father." Hope says, "Disappointment will not shackle my season. Instead, my resolute hope makes room for joy, which will mark my days." Hope stares in the eyes of the enemy and shouts of the eternal reward the Father offers through his Son.

Relentless hope in Jesus is not naive, nor is it ignorant of tricky circumstances. We grow stronger, not by our own accomplishments or mastery, but by the death and resurrection of Jesus. We stand with a thousand generations and hold unswervingly to the hope of life in Christ. We walk in His promises. We claim His inheritance. We dance in the fullness of God.

CHAPTER ELEVEN

Loss

*L*oss is a broken relationship. It is the death of a child. It is grieving a parent you never knew. It is losing your job or your family. It is losing a way and rhythm of life that you once knew but will never know again. Loss makes us question the good gospel we've come to believe. We wonder if God's promises can be true when we lose a well-loved person or well-lived season. Loss soaks our hearts with grief. More grief than we ever bargained for. It redefines how we view our lives and the lives of others. The undeniable nature of loss gives us no wiggle room to believe for a different outcome. The grief of loss is weighty. Sometimes we make big decisions about who we believe God is when we are in our moments of deep loss.

After four months in Uganda, we arrived home to the Pacific Northwest amidst fanfare and celebration. It was a sunny July afternoon when we returned, and we touched ground at the same airport that I had arrived at twenty-four years earlier on my flight to my new home in the United States from India. After twenty hours of flying, followed by interviews at customs, I couldn't believe it was truly over. No more clutching him tightly for fear something would change in our case and the powers that be would snatch him away. No more hoping. No more waiting. No more wondering if I would never see him again. We stood on American soil with our son. We were a family. It was officially written on paper with Ugandan courts, with United States immigration, and on the tablet of our hearts.

Overstimulated by all the attention, our sweet Jericho flashed silly smiles between yawns to dozens of family and friends. So many who'd rallied around us in prayer and donations were gathered at the airport, anxious to meet the fruit of their intercession. There were hugs, kisses, and happy tears. It stands as one of the most sacred moments of my life.

I watched a fuzzy VHS of my adoption homecoming countless times while I was growing up. That VHS tape was the only evidence I had of my beginning, and I loved it. I wanted my son to have the same gift, so I hired a film crew to document our arrival and our dedication, right there in the airport, smack dab in the middle of baggage claim. It was perfect. There is so much goodness and grace tucked in those moments. I treasure them in my heart.

Day by day we offer our sadness, and the
Good Lord gives us strength to see life
revived after loss.

My mind wanted to believe everything would be alright. The hard part was most definitely over. We were home. We were a family now. Nothing could get us down. Right?

I was sorely mistaken.

What we lose in the dark must be found in the Light.

Parenting Jericho six thousand miles *away* from my home looked a lot different than parenting him *in* my home. Plus, Lucius was gone. He would always be thousands of miles away. I would have given anything to sneak one more hug. One more giggle. One more kiss. My heart ached. On one hand, I was overcome with joy over Jericho. But on the other hand, I was also buckling under the weight of my loss. My Lucius.

Still, Jericho, day by day, blossomed into the boy God intended. His young soul processed his own losses: missing Lucius and everything else he knew as normal. Starting over is never easy and especially not when you are only two and a half. As he settled into our family he tried to share as best as he could, what he missed. Together, we mourned what he lost. We didn't gloss over the hard parts. We didn't pretend. We leaned into the painful memories. We felt the loss.

Paula Rinehart writes in *Strong Women, Soft Hearts*:

> At the center of being a woman lies a paradox that can help us understand why we often find living from the heart a precarious venture.
>
> On one hand, we possess a rather wonderful capacity for relationship. Our language is that of the heart—experiencing life deeply, feeling connected to those we love, enjoying the ambiance. This capacity enriches our lives immeasurably. That's the good news.
>
> The bad news is that this very capacity also makes us more vulnerable to loss. You can't make a relationship happen like you would make up your mind to start a business or achieve some tangible goal. Relationships, and really most matters of the heart, are inherently more unmanageable. Relationships defy our attempts at control. The people we love don't always love us back. Friends move away. Lovers change. And the truth is that if we live long enough, we face the potential loss of everyone who matters to us.
>
> So the very capacity that provides our ticket to the richest moments of life—to the most meaningful connection with God and with those we love—also riddles our lives with risk. Our greatest capacity for relationship opens up a larger possibility

for experiencing pain. The secret of our hearts is that we can be touched. We can be moved deeply. Simply put, *we can be gotten to.*[1]

The effects of loss will not go away on their own. We must be willing to accept the reality of loss. No matter how big or how small. No one gets to downplay or exaggerate our losses. They are real losses and they are ours. We mourn for our losses. We mourn for ourselves. Mourning in itself is a good and healthy act. It lets us recognize what our heart will never get back. What will never be recovered. If we handle our hearts with delicate care, we can breathe new life where only grief consumed us.

Acquainted with Our Grief

If we avoid grieving our losses we find ourselves sliding down a sharp slope of despair. In our effort to escape pain we may find our hearts in more pain than we planned. We can't cheat the grieving process. It won't work. We have permission to weep. Our tears make way for what's to come as they wash our hearts clean of pain-filled memories. We ache in our lament and that's OK. We mourn, not from lack of faith, but from love. In John 11, Jesus shared a tender moment with Mary and Martha over the death of their brother and Jesus' friend, Lazarus. He wept. He had plans to revive brother Lazarus but wept with the sisters in Scripture before the miracle of resurrection. He didn't hide His tears or pretend everything was all right. With those dear women, He leaned into the loss and mourned.

Like us, sisters Mary and Martha were subject to the capriciousness of this world. They couldn't prevent calamity and were reminded that life is full of hardship and loss. Life is bittersweet. There is no way to escape the corporeal ways of the world. While they marveled at

Christ's resurrection power, the gift made plain to us in John 11 is the nearness and the way Jesus shared in their grief. He didn't tell them to stop weeping. He didn't tell them their pain didn't matter, because it did. The pain mattered to Mary and Martha and it mattered to Him. We see our Savior, once again, acquainted with our grief.

Loss that left us rejected twenty, thirty, or forty years ago has the potential to be the source of a grace and a glory we never knew possible.

In loss, what we love is taken from us. We know in those grief-stricken times that we are people with a great capacity to love one another. Our grief is the proof. As we learn how to live our lives after loss, the Holy Spirit gives us space to receive. We find blessings tangled in our grief. Day by day we offer our sadness, and the Good Lord gives us strength to see life revived after loss. He reminds us that we are still breathing, still moving, and the sun is still rising. He is with us as memories return to our minds. He is with us as we refocus our life on the relationships we have. He will refresh our vision to help us see that life is still full and whole in Him. In Him alone. The enemy may try to trick us into believing that if we move on, it means we didn't truly love what we had. The enemy accuses us of disloyalty. It's a lie. We are capable of loving well and then of moving on.

There is such relief from loss when you are able to recall all you have lost without an incapacitating pit in your stomach. That is when you know it is well with your soul. That is when your grief no longer steals your energy and saps your joy. The loss remains an event in your life, but that event is not one that defines the rest of your life.

It may be scary to love again, whether it is another man, another child, another friend, or even God. Yet, if we scheme to protect ourselves from future losses we will lose out on love. That vivacious kind of love that reminds us that God is good, God is overflowing with love. Psalm 94:19 reads, "In the multitude of my anxieties within me, / Your comforts delight my soul" (NKJV).

In our worst loss, God is there. He is not absent. Like you, I have friends who have experienced miscarriages, stillborn births, or the death of their own children. They have suffered the sting of divorce, the passing of a parent, or the shattering of a friendship. Each and every time that loss shakes up our world. The only way through the grief is to ask the Lord for His hand of comfort. It is His presence that gives you the gumption to show up to your own life.

God took on the form of man to share in our lives of flesh and blood. He wants to share our joy and our sorrow. Christ is no stranger to loss. He does not sit idly by in situations of grief. Instead, He steps forward to commune with us in our triumphs and our tragedies.

I could not foresee how the loss of Lucius would rip open other losses I had experienced in my life. I felt again the deep pain from the loss of the mother I had never met. I did not even know what she looked like. Did I have her eyes? Her nose? I was a mother now, which meant she was a grandmother, and she didn't even know it. I wanted her to know God was good to me. I wanted her to know I didn't blame her or shame her for her choice to give me away. I wanted her to know I loved her. I wanted her to taste the forgiving and grace-filled gospel of Jesus. Sadly, I knew that she would never know these thoughts and feelings that bounced around in my mind. I grieved again as a mother myself. I grieved the loss of a woman I had never met, and that loss drove me once again to the feet of Jesus.

Other losses from my past didn't torture me. Instead, they pointed me to the goodness and the hand of God. When we receive new blessings—most notably our union with Christ—we receive redemption from our past grief. God is a redeemer of broken moments, both past and present. He is not subject to our limits of time and space. Loss that left us rejected twenty, thirty, or forty years ago has the potential to be the source of a grace and a glory we never knew possible. If we want to turn our loss to light, it means we must make our way through our loss.

Our loss may leave us confused and alone. Loss makes us worry about what more we may lose in our lives. In those delicate times, the kind Holy Spirit guides us through every wave of grief. If we are attentive to every feeling, learning from every emotion, we will find that life carries on. Not exactly as it was but as something new. Beauty rises from ashes. Christ's death and resurrection is our testament to new days, new seasons, and renewed lives. Psalm 30:11-12a reads:

> You have turned my mourning into joyful dancing.
>> You have taken away my clothes of mourning and clothed
>> me with joy,
> that I might sing praises to you and not be silent (NLT).

His comfort and presence make way for His blessings as we mourn. When we address our losses, whether from a year ago or twenty years ago, we won't be tormented but blessed. Richly blessed. Psalm 18:28 informs us, "You, LORD, keep my lamp burning; / my God turns my darkness into light." Our darkness is no match for His light. Our loss is no match for His love.

Dreams Redeemed

Six months after we arrived home from Uganda, with the rituals of toddler parenting settling into the no-pattern pattern that is common of life with a three-year-old, I felt myself slowly piecing my heart back together. I was finding a way to cope with the loss of Lucius and the reminders of my missing mother. My body was healing by God's tender hand. I felt different. Different enough, in fact, that I purchased a home pregnancy test.

At 6:45 in the morning, two faint lines, to my surprise, flashed bright red. As we scrambled to get ready for work, I told Derek the news. He was elated. He danced around the room as he brushed his teeth, repeating, "Are you sure? Are you sure?" He immediately recognized God's graceful hand in our lives, but I met God with questioning. Is this going to be impossible odds? My journey to motherhood had not been the easiest trek of my life so far. How would this part go? We had been planning to expand our family, but two kids in eighteen months? Sure, they would be four years apart. Still, it suddenly seemed like more than I could handle. Lies of the enemy crept into my heart, reminding me of my failure to mother two sons. Anxiety took my every breath.

Over time, probably longer than I expected, I accepted my new reality and growing bump. At my twenty-week ultrasound, I was eager to see the sex of my baby. While I had a coat of gooey jelly on my belly, the technician took pictures of every angle before the big reveal. With a white-knuckle grip on Derek's hand, I listened as she said, "Your son has a baby brother."

I was speechless. What I lost, God chose to return. I do not believe that in every loss we will find a blessing that so directly redeems what we have lost, but I do believe the Lord knows our hearts completely.

He is speaking to us in our loss. He is fluent in the language of love and care. He sees our tears. He does not miss our grieving moments. My husband spotted God's hand relatively early in our new season, but it took me a little longer. I found it in the sterile doctor's office. The God of all creation knew my story. He had a plan for new life. His sovereign, grace-giving hand was upon me. I felt peace.

Another twenty weeks later, after forty hours of labor, I met my second son. This one was a child of my flesh and blood. He had my thick curly hair. He had my bright brown eyes. He was a gift, a reminder of God's goodness and glory. I named him Kingston. A son of the kingdom of God.

After death comes new life. Maybe it is the death of a dream. Maybe it is the death of a relationship. Loss of a job, a child, a parent. After the dead of winter, new life springs forth. We have new breath. His Spirit aids in our regenerated life.

We are not in charge of our stories, although many of us would not mind assuming the role of captain of the ship. There is already a Captain far superior who navigates the waves and storms we encounter. He is faithful and true. He is a Comforter. He is a Giver of new life. He is a Restorer of lost and broken moments. He is a Giver of blessings. Blessings beyond what we can fathom or imagine on our own. He is with us.

Very Good News

Our losses are not only our own. Jesus takes them on with us as His own. He accepts the sorrow they bring. He weeps. He mourns. He holds us through our grief. He gives us space to wrestle with our heavy emotions. He is patient and kind. Comforting and peaceful. He is the light at the end of the tunnel. The one we've been waiting for.

Isaiah 61:1-3 says:

> The Spirit of the Sovereign LORD is on me,
>> because the LORD has anointed me
>> to proclaim good news to the poor.
> He has sent me to bind up the brokenhearted,
>> to proclaim freedom for the captives
>> and release from darkness for the prisoners,
> to proclaim the year of the LORD's favor
>> and the day of vengeance of our God,
> to comfort all who mourn,
>> and provide for those who grieve in Zion—
> to bestow on them a crown of beauty
>> instead of ashes,
> the oil of joy
>> instead of mourning,
> and a garment of praise
>> instead of a spirit of despair.
> They will be called oaks of righteousness,
>> a planting of the LORD
>> for the display of his splendor.

The poor. The brokenhearted. The captives. The prisoners. The common denominator woven through each of these groups is loss. The good news of Jesus is for those of us who have lost precious people and a treasured way of life. The good news of Jesus is for those who are alone and wondering if good will come out of their circumstances. It's a love song for humanity that restores and gives jubilant blessing instead of despair. The good news of Jesus is a radiant crown of beauty for our smoldering ashes. Our King gives us the blessing of unspeakable joy, which we could never give to ourselves. He delivers us from our sin, our shame, our rejection, and our loss. He is without end. He is full of compassion, grace, and peace when we have lost what matters most to us.

MacLaren's Expositions explains Isaiah 61:3:

> Jesus Christ transforms sorrow because he transforms the mourner. How does He do this? One answer to that question is by giving to the man with ashes on his head and gloom wrapped about his spirit, sources of joy, if he will use them, altogether independent of external circumstances. Though the fig-tree shall not blossom, and there be no fruit in the vine . . . yet will I rejoice in the Lord. And every Christian man, especially when days are dark and clouds are gathering, has it open to him, and is bound to use the possibility, to turn away his mind from the external occasions of sadness, and fix it on the changeless reason for deep and unchanging joy—the sweet presence, the strong love, the sustaining hand, the infinite wisdom, of his Father God.
>
> Brethren, "the paradox of the Christian life" is, "as sorrowful, yet always rejoicing." Christ calls for no hypocritical insensibility to "the ills that flesh is heir to." He has sanctioned by His example the tears that flow when death hurts loving hearts. He commanded the women of Jerusalem to "weep for themselves and for their children." He means that we should feel the full bitterness and pain of sorrows which will not be medicinal unless they are bitter, and will not be curative unless they cut deep. But He also means that whilst thus we suffer as men, in the depths of our own hearts we should, at the same time, be turning away from the sufferings and their cause, and fixing our hearts, quiet even then amidst the distractions, upon God Himself. Ah! it is hard to do, and because we do not do it, the promise that He will turn the sorrow into joy often seems to be a vain word for us.[2]

In our loss, we can cling to Christ. When we taste the sour punch of loss, we can't go on as usual, and our hearts demand answers. We can cling to Christ. When the illusion of control and ease is gone. We can cling to Christ. Our grief, while tragic, attunes our ears to hear the heartbeat of the Father. We can climb into his lap and listen to his promises of peace. His promises of freedom. His promises of blessing. Our blessings raise us above the ashes of our grief.

He is acquainted with our searing loss and our debilitating grief. He will draw us near, hold us close, and give us jubilant joy at just the right time.

Twenty years ago, I met Ruby. I was ten years old when she spotted me sitting under a tree in the summer heat of St. Louis at a gathering of adopted children from India. Alone with my thoughts in the shade, I was overwhelmed by meeting other children who looked like me. For once I was in the majority of those around me, but I still felt out of place. As I struggled to feel a sense of belonging, I heard a tender voice call me, "Abhilasha." I perked up at the sound of a name I'd only seen written on my adoption decree. Ruby, the dark-skinned and brown-eyed woman who spoke to me, explained that she was the caretaker of the orphanage where I had been taken as an infant. My young heart was overwhelmed by the experience. We exchanged pleasantries but not much more.

Twenty years later I met Ruby at a coffee shop in Seattle. For years she had been looking for me and finally had tracked me down through mutual connections I didn't even know we had. The same tender voice called me by name, "Abhilasha." This time, instead of a quick exchange, we hugged and chatted like old friends. She explained, "All I wanted was for you to know the life-saving knowledge of Jesus Christ." I fought back tears as I responded with a simple, "Yes, I love Him so much."

As our conversation progressed, she shared details of my story I had never known before. In the fall of 1986, she had had a burning desire to care for a baby. As the caretaker of an orphanage with dozens of children in her custody, she knew this longing must be from the Lord. Then, at two days old, I was brought to her, the baby she had longed for. She named me Abhilasha, which in Hindi means *desire*. She held me, cuddled me, bathed me, and cared for me as her own. God's hand of grace revealed through her words astounded me. I drove home in silence and then wept on my couch for hours. That day I fell in love with Jesus all over again. He was present in my loss. I knew without a shadow of a doubt that His hand had been on me from the minute I was born and that He is exactly who He says He is—a loving God full of grace and truth.

Everyday Blessings

For me, God's blessing looks like a toothy smile from my chunky toddler whenever he sees me. It's the look in his eyes when I walk in the door as he flails his arms and legs to make his way onto my lap. It's the nuzzle on my neck and the grip of his chubby little fingers. It's the way he calls out, "Mama, Mama, Mama," when he's scared or anxious. He wants my presence. He wants my affection. He wants my touch. That in itself is a blessing.

I'm aware of little, daily blessings that might have gone unnoticed if I had not experienced loss. My little lamb chop feels happiest in the company of me, his brother, and his beloved daddy. He giggles, coos, and jabbers most when I'm with him, just the two of us. A strange person or unfamiliar environment causes him to hold me closer, never letting me out of his sight. He isn't shy about his need and desire to be in my presence. He can't help himself. He is most himself when with me. While this may sound like normal development to most parents, it is different from my experiences with my firstborn. When your first child is adopted these aren't run-of-the-mill experiences you have in your home. These moments, these blessings, with Kingston were new.

Both my kids have taught me so much about the love, nearness, and sovereignty of Father God. With Jericho, I bore witness to a familiar trauma that happens when you remove the presence of a mother, the presence of care and protection, the promise of love and provision. When a child is left alone, anxiety and rage can quickly shackle the soul. Abandonment wreaks havoc on the heart. When that child is placed in a family, intentional bonding reworks what's been broken, and little blessings bloom like spring's first buds even in what first appeared as desolate soil.

I've seen Jericho find his footing, stand strong in his identity, and come alive, but not without heartache. I had no idea the feelings of loss that rattled my heart would one day echo out of my own son's mouth. I had no idea that he, too, would be convinced that others with Olan Mills baby pictures were happier than He could ever be. I, also, had no idea it would be so hard to convince him otherwise. But I should have known. I should have known he, too, would wonder where his tummy mama was. He, too, would feel shame for the color of his skin and the beginning of his story. I should have been ready because I had been there myself, with the same thoughts and the same loss. Yet, daily blessings are found even after devastating loss.

No matter what our loss is, we can find our solace and blessing in our Savior.

One of my great encouragements in times of grief is the words from the old Irish hymn "Be Thou My Vision":

> High King of heaven, my victory won,
> may I reach heaven's joys, O bright heaven's sun!
> Heart of my own heart, whatever befall,
> still be my vision, O Ruler of all.[3]

Our Good Father holds us close. His presence gives rest to our souls in anguish. All will be well with our heart when we have relinquished our rights to Him. He is acquainted with our searing loss and our debilitating grief. He will draw us near, hold us close, and give us jubilant joy at just the right time. When we confront our dark moments, He will be the blazing candle we couldn't light on our own. We will thrive in the fellowship of His death and resurrection as we follow Him, as we set Him as our True North. Our vision in and out of season. No matter what our lives look like, let us be washed in the blessings of God's presence, His love, and our ever desperate need for Him.

CHAPTER TWELVE

Fear

*H*ave you ever been so consumed by fear that you can hardly think straight? I certainly have been. It seems the older I get, the more things I discover that incite fear in me: fear of a plane crash (check), fear of my husband and children dying (check), fear of being alone (check), fear of humiliation (check), fear of genetically modified food that will mess with my innards (check), fear of failure (check), fear of dying young (check), and fear of a house fire (check). Like you, if there's a catastrophe that will alter the course of my life, I've feared it.

We are so paralyzed by our fear that the abundant and vibrant life we are meant to live sits buried under a mound of worry. We convince ourselves that we aren't hurting anyone by fearing the worst, that we're just realists, right? Our worry becomes threaded into the tapestry of our personality; it is part of what we believe about ourselves and who we will become in this life.

Stasi Eldridge says, "Fear is a wet blanket that smothers the fiery passion God deposited in your heart when he formed you. Fear freezes us into inaction. Frozen ideas, frozen souls, frozen bodies can't move, can't dream, can't risk, can't love, and can't live. Fear chains us."[1] For our lives to be all they were destined to be, it requires us to think differently. Our faith necessitates that we fight fear. Fear takes the best out of us, and faith only adds to what God has already done. Without question, fear and faith are opposites. They don't commingle. They won't ever be caught dancing together.

One draws us closer to the Father and the other scoots us away. In every case of fear, Father God is not the source or author. He is the answer to conquering it.

Fear is a clever tactic that the enemy has used since the beginning of time. He twists our questions into worries that leave us paralyzed and isolated in our own minds. Fear highlights every past mistake, every loss, every event that would bolster its argument. We believe that if we are confronted with our worst fears we will not possibly survive. It's the biggest lie the enemy throws our way. It's his same old song and dance. We pay admission and eat up his nasty rhetoric. We believe the hype that fear propagates in our thoughts. The enemy wins when we entertain our fears. It digs up the deeply planted roots of our faith.

Whenever we fear, we resign our power to the object of that fear. Be it our abuser, accuser, or joy-stealer. We sometimes become consumed in such a shadowed life that we expect our worst fears to come true, even though many of our fears will *never* materialize. Some of them will. We cannot control how it all unfolds. When we are fixated on worry, we do not make space to worship and trust the One who is worthy. Our souls cannot survive only being fed a steady diet of dread.

The Unknown

After we became a family of four, again, I sensed a big change for our family. Something new. To be honest, I didn't have a crystal-clear picture of what it would look like. I knew that our next step would bring along with it profound change for our family. What I thought was going to be a carefree transition became my opportunity to face my biggest fears: my fear of lack, losing security, and standing up for what's right even in the midst of opposition. In the throes of change, I didn't understand that on the other side of fear, the Lord had already prepared a space for me. A space to trust Him in ways I never had before. Overcome by His provision—His presence and His promises —I had no excuses. It was time to stretch my faith.

He didn't ask Derek or me to play it safe. There was no promise of ease. No promise of stability. The only promise was His presence and the challenge toward a God-sized portion of faith. With courage, He asked us to follow Him along this unknown path. To give up everything we'd relied on in the past and to set our sights on the season ahead. Our 401(k), health insurance, church, employment, and friends weren't the heroes of our story. Jesus solely was.

Both my husband and I left the jobs we'd worked hard at and poured our hearts into for seven years. Everything that God had given us freely as a blessing, He asked us to give up. We chose to trust Him, even though we felt afraid and intimidated. We wondered how we'd pay the mortgage, how our children would handle so much change. To find a new school for my son, new jobs for me and my husband, and a new church for all of us was enough to make anyone anxious.

Trust Issues

Fear serves as an alarm; it's flashing red light registers that somewhere there is a lack of receiving and trusting love. The love only Christ gives. First John 4:18 tells us, "Such love has no fear, because perfect love expels all fear. If we are afraid, it is for fear of punishment, and this shows that we have not fully experienced his perfect love" (NLT).

Quite some time ago, a friend sent me this verse, and it left me scratching my head. How could love drive out fear? How could love dislodge every worry cemented into the foundation of my soul? It's only when we play out our worst fears and find they won't destroy us that we see the power of love. The love of Christ will pick us up. The same love that sent Jesus to the cross will give us the courage to carry on. We will not be destroyed by our fears, because by the power of His love, Jesus fully paid the price to deliver us from each and every one of them.

We will not be destroyed by our fears, because by the power of His love, Jesus fully paid the price to deliver us from each and every one of them.

Such peace springs from the ultimate understanding that we are His beloved daughters. We belong to a Father who doesn't allow fear to determine the story line. The story was always intended to be one of love. The greatest love story ever told. A grand adventure where the Father sent His Son to rescue you. For your heart. For your soul. For goodness in and through your one precious life. All because of his lavish love.

Isaiah 41:13 reminds us,

> For I am the LORD your God
> who takes hold of your right hand
> and says to you, Do not fear;
> I will help you.

God spoke these words through the prophet Isaiah to the frightened people of Israel. He gave them the same encouragement He offers today: fear not. He will always help us if we place our trust in Him. In fear, we are reminded more than ever, we need God; we find out how small we are and how vast the power and grace of God is. We can't escape the torment of our fears without Him. The tireless master of fear won't give up on us. He will pursue us to the very ends of the earth.

Although the most debilitating season of fear that I've experienced is long past, I'm shocked at just how hard the enemy continues to gnaw away on us. In a season in which God had been good to my family, in which blessings, both big and small, popped up like daisies, I again sensed fear competing to take center stage. To play the starring role in my story. It is not just in hard times we contend with fear; it is also in times of beauty and rest. In new opportunities, accomplishments, and new beginnings, fear capitalizes the moment and seeks to cast its pall over all the beauty.

The Good Lord knew we'd wrestle with fear as it attempts to hijack the narrative of grace, healing, wholeness, forgiveness, and courage written in our stories. He offers us safekeeping where fear cannot hurt or harm us—where it can't even reach us. Psalm 91:1-2 says,

> He who dwells in the shelter of the Most High
> Will abide in the shadow of the Almighty.
> I will say to the LORD, "My refuge and my fortress,
> My God, in whom I trust!" (NASB)

Our trust in God allows us access to rest and safety; He is a refuge and fortress. A fortress is inaccessible, this space so well protected an enemy could not approach it—there is supreme safety in Christ.

The enemy hurls fears our way in hopes we'll lose trust in God. If we take the bait, we lose trust in the Father. We forget the abundant courage afforded by His extravagant love. We leave the fortress, subject to the brutal and relentless assault of fear. May we never forget: fear is fought through active trust, with belief in the goodness, power, and sovereignty of God.

Do Not Be Afraid

The most widely hailed woman in all of history is a hero of the faith who trusted implicitly in God's plan and timing. A woman who gave up her reputation for a God-ordained life of sacrifice and love. A woman who fought fear with faith. A woman whose courage we talk about to this very day. Her name is Mary, mother of Jesus.

Luke 1:26-38 shares the beginning of her story:

> In the sixth month of Elizabeth's pregnancy, God sent the angel Gabriel to Nazareth, a town in Galilee, to a virgin pledged to be married to a man named Joseph, a descendant of David. The virgin's name was Mary. The angel went to her and said, "Greetings, you who are highly favored! The Lord is with you."
>
> Mary was greatly troubled at his words and wondered what kind of greeting this might be. But the angel said to her, "Do not be afraid, Mary; you have found favor with God. You will conceive and give birth to a son, and you are to call him Jesus. He will be great and will be called the Son of the Most High. The Lord God will give him the throne of his father David, and he will reign over Jacob's descendants forever; his kingdom will never end."
>
> "How will this be," Mary asked the angel, "since I am a virgin?"

The angel answered, "The Holy Spirit will come on you, and the power of the Most High will overshadow you. So the holy one to be born will be called the Son of God. Even Elizabeth your relative is going to have a child in her old age, and she who was said to be unable to conceive is in her sixth month. For no word from God will ever fail."

"I am the Lord's servant," Mary answered. "May your word to me be fulfilled." Then the angel left her.

Mary, at the appearance and greeting of Gabriel, was terrified. His second exchange with her was, "Do not be afraid, Mary; you have found favor with God." I don't imagine his command wiped out the fear that was coursing through her veins, but he explained, with the favor of the Father, there was no reason to fear. Gabriel knew fear would do its best to dissolve hope in God's glorious plan for Mary's life. Fear is particularly present on the brink of miracles, promise, revealed hope, delight, and beauty.

Our girl Mary would never be the same after her brief visit with the angel Gabriel. She would never bounce along, carefree, and enjoy anonymity, keeping to herself. No, she'd never enjoy a quiet life alone with her husband. The agenda of heaven stripped her of her earthly comforts and plans. Her virginity, which in her time was equated to her worth as a woman and her value to her family, would be questioned. It wasn't simply a matter of anatomy or purity in that culture; it was a matter of identity. She'd be seen as damaged goods and have no opportunities for inclusion in that society if she lost her virginity. What mattered as a sign to others and herself, she would forfeit.

However, Mary was favored by the King of kings. She was chosen for great works that would serve not only her own soul but also everyone throughout human history. What's so wild is that before she was filled with the Holy Spirit and overshadowed by the Most High, before she gave birth to the Son of God, she declared to Gabriel, "I am the Lord's servant. . . . May your word to me be fulfilled." She chose to trust in the promised God of love. She chose courage, not fear, as her companion for the journey ahead.

Fear of embarrassment, stoning, or being left by her fiancé could've stolen the story that unfolded. But it didn't. Bravery won. Mary believed that God was who He'd declared He was. She believed in His power. She believed He would follow through on His plans, never to fail. The greatest bravery is trust in the love and power of God. It's not digging deep and trying to find power sourced in ourselves. It's only in the very One who created us, loves us, and rescues us.

Author Donald Miller writes:

> The most often repeated commandment in the Bible is "Do not fear." It's in there over two hundred times. That means a couple of things, if you think about it. It means we are going to be afraid, and it means we shouldn't let fear boss us around. Before I realized we were supposed to fight fear, I thought of fear as a subtle suggestion in our subconscious designed to keep us safe, or more important, keep us from getting humiliated. And I guess it serves that purpose. But fear isn't only a guide to keep us safe; it's also a manipulative emotion that can trick us into living a boring life.[2]

Fear of failure, humiliation, degradation, and loneliness keeps us from embarking on the boldest God-sized dreams of our hearts. It cuts us off at the knees. Bravery is found in the refuge and fortress of the Almighty. Bravery gives our weary hearts and bodies the good sense to silence the accuser and father of lies, who looks to destroy us with our fears. When we face our fears, we make the greatest gains in life. We see God most victorious in our lives as we let Him handle our fears with His gift of courage. It makes a way for us to face the uncertainty and move forward with the rest of our story.

Triggers

Some time ago, I felt paralyzed with fear and it took fresh perspective to remember my faithful Savior has reliably never left me alone. In a season of struggle, I agonized over my worrisome heart more than I ever thought I would. I let my fears rule the roost. They poked holes at my deep reverence and trust in Jesus. When my dread got the best of me, the good Lord gave me a fiery friend to remind me how to get through the fear-filled days. At a brow appointment. Of which I am a regular attendee (listen, I'm an East Indian woman with facial hair for days. I'd resemble a distant relative of Bigfoot if it wasn't for the magic worked by my soul sister of an aesthetician). Years ago, my dear friend, Jessica, who's waxed my face for the past six years, became one of my closest companions. Her radical faith, grip on grace, and sage-like wisdom made their mark on me every time I sat in her comfy spa chair.

He is fully able, no matter the size or complication of our fears, to swap them with his full assurance of power and love.

As the hot wax coated my face, I spilled my story, one darkened by the shackles of fear. I explained that I'd melt into a puddle if I faced the fears that tortured my already tender heart. She looked straight into my eyes and with a stern voice said, "No." She smacked my hand and declared, "That's not the life God has for you. Here's what you'll do when you have a trigger, when you spot your worst fear headed straight for the center of your heart, you'll shout the truth from the belly of your soul. You weren't made for fear, Tiffany. You were made for faith."

She went on to share passages, many of which I've listed in this chapter, to combat the sharp tongue of fear. Our world gets small, real quick, when fear starts crowding out the good and glorious faith God builds.

It's true. We're made for faith. Fear from the enemy, and thoughts not taken captive for the good will of God, will eat us if we let them. To exchange fear for faith, we have to believe God is for us. He is faithful. Always available for us. Lamentations 3:22-23 encourages us,

> Because of the LORD's great love we are not consumed,
>> for his compassions never fail.
> They are new every morning;
>> great is your faithfulness.

His faithfulness won't abandon us when we need it most, especially when we're shaking in our shiny boots. He's all-powerful. He uses that power for our good. Isaiah 40:29 tells us, "He gives power to the weak / and strength to the powerless" (NLT).

There's no use trying to "man up" and lift up what weighs us down. It's Christ who does the heavy lifting in our lives. We can't manage this on our own in a way that prompts deep connection with God. If we sorted it ourselves we wouldn't need a Savior. It's properly handled when we slide our chair up close to Christ and tell Him the truth. Our honesty with Him grows our dependency on Him. We present our fears to Him. He sees them one by one. Our fear of abandonment. Our fear of lack. Our fear of humiliation. Our fear of losing the ones we love most. Our fear of betrayal. He can handle it all. He is fully able, no matter the size or complication of our fears, to swap them with his full assurance of power and love.

After we pitch our fears, we wash in the truth of His words. We let it permeate our heart and mind until it leaks from every corner of our being. Isaiah 54:10 says,

> "Though the mountains be shaken
>   and the hills be removed,
> yet my unfailing love for you will not be shaken
>   nor my covenant of peace be removed,"
>   says the LORD, who has compassion on you.

If His unfailing love is ours, it is a love so sacred with means to demolish our worry. What we need we already have. His love, brimming with power, trumps any fear the enemy heaves our way. No matter where we are, or what we are doing, we can recall the promises of heaven through our prayerful worship to cast out frantic fear. In worship, we praise God until we believe his promises.

You aren't bound by your fears in such a way that would somehow render God helpless to redeem your nerve-wracked self.

The situations, which trigger our fears, may not change, but we do. It's our heart, bolstered by the confidence we have in the goodness and love of God that enables us to walk through potentially fearful days. It's our trust in the Father that unlocks our solid security. We aren't promised smooth sailing, but we can sail the high seas with the full assurance of Christ's presence and promises.

Ephesians 6:10-17 instructs us:

> Finally, be strong in the Lord and in his mighty power. Put on the full armor of God, so that you can take your stand against the devil's schemes. For our struggle is not against flesh and blood, but against the rulers, against the authorities, against the powers of this dark world and against the spiritual forces of evil in the heavenly realms. Therefore put on the full armor of God, so that when the day of evil comes, you may be able to stand your ground, and after you have done everything, to stand. Stand firm then, with the belt of truth buckled around your waist, with the breastplate of righteousness in place, and with your feet fitted with the readiness that comes from the gospel of peace. In addition to all this, take up the shield of faith, with which you can extinguish all the flaming arrows of the evil one. Take the helmet of salvation and the sword of the Spirit, which is the word of God.

The armor of God protects us from the enemy's game plan. In truth, righteousness, and peace we stand firm. It's the shield of faith, not fear, that "extinguishes all the flaming arrows of the evil one." The armor and shields explained in Ephesians protected every inch of the body. The shields left no spot exposed to the invading army. Any dart is harmless. Yet, the shield of faith only works if we use it. If we leave it by the wayside we'll be sitting ducks. It's our faith, our communion with Christ and His ways, that keep the enemy's shady tricks from destroying our souls.

The Honest Truth

I tell you now, living in fear provides no advantages for brave, Jesus-loving women; fear has kept us from doing the right thing, the hard thing, far too many times. Fear only has the power we choose to give it. Bravery is a much better option. Bravery says we'll fight for what we believe in, remain vulnerable with those we trust, and boldly walk in the fullness of God. As we fold laundry, negotiate in meetings, trod out to our lunch date, wrangle those kids, have the hard conversation with a friend, and take a moment to ourselves, remember, we were born for this. We were born to thrive in life. Bravery in Christ makes a way. We don't fight the current of fear but remove ourselves completely from it.

I don't know when fear finds you, but it sneaks up on me most often when I'm alone. It's when my thoughts get to me. It's when I'm tired. Feeling weak. Since having kids, my fear meter has gone through the roof. In those moments, I take a deep breath and let the words from 2 Timothy 1:7—"For God has not given us a spirit of fear and timidity, but of power, love, and self-discipline" (NLT)—ring true over my noisy heart. What's given from the Father—power, love, and self-discipline—are for my good and growth. They are gifts for the journey. Ones I can't live without.

Fear did its absolute best to cut me off at the knees, rob me of opportunity, and keep me safe on the shore, far from Christ's invitation to swim in the deep fullness He has for me. I would never be the woman God destined if I let my fear of abandonment, fear of losing security and love, fear of being a horrid mother, or fear of what others think lead my thoughts. I believe the same for you. Although we feel justified in our worry, we are most certainly not justified. Our suspicion of the worst is a detour from our story of wholeness and redemption.

Dear sister, you aren't a coward. You aren't bound by your fears in such a way that would somehow render God helpless to redeem your nerve-wracked self. He is faithful, powerful, and sovereign. May His tender, sure, and firm grip on your shoulder assure you that you aren't riding solo. The Shepherd goes before you. The Rescuer rides in on His white horse, with love and truth.

Take the fearful thoughts captive. Offer them to the Redeemer. He will be faithful to exchange your fear with love, hope, and bravery. He won't fail you. He won't hang you out to dry. He brought you this far and intends to lead you forward. He's got your back; He holds the good future. He won't betray you. Won't hornswoggle you out of what your soul deeply desires.

Your own soul and the world around you crave freedom from fear. If you let fear win, you'll miss out on the great journey God hand-crafted for you. The adventure of wild trust, seeing His inexplicable plans come to fruition. You'll miss out on miracles, the kind you could never conjure up on your own. You'll miss out on bravery, love, and power. Others will see the greatness and glory of Jesus because you rose up to be the beloved and fierce woman God forged you to be.

If fear won, Moses wouldn't have led the Israelites across the Red Sea. If fear won, Noah wouldn't have built the ark. If fear won, Esther wouldn't have approached Xerxes. If fear won, Abraham wouldn't be the father of many nations. If fear won, Deborah wouldn't have led her army to victory over the Canaanites. If fear won, Gideon wouldn't have defeated the Midianites. If fear won, we wouldn't know the strength, grace, and victory of those who've gone before us, offering us living proof that God is for us.

You may not slay an opposing army or witness the Red Sea part, but you'll face fear; and by the power of God, you'll see your fear crumble before you. You'll flourish in this present day. May your choice be rooted in power and love. For this is the way to live. May freedom, joy, belief, love, hope, grace, and truth sprout in your soul as you walk in the fullness of God. Because you, my darling, are never alone.

Notes

1. Shame

1. Brené Brown, *Daring Greatly: How the Courage to Be Vulnerable Transforms the Way We Live, Love, Parent, and Lead* (New York: Gotham, 2012), 67.

2. Doubt

1. Christine Caine, *Living Life Undaunted: 365 Readings and Reflections from Christine Caine* (Grand Rapids: Zondervan, 2014), 132.

2. Dan B. Allender and Tremper Longman, *The Cry of the Soul: How Our Emotions Reveal Our Deepest Questions About God* (Colorado Springs: NavPress, 1994), 25.

3. Isolation

1. Brennan Manning, *Abba's Child: The Cry of the Heart for Intimate Belonging* (Colorado Springs: NavPress, 2015), 6.

2. Henry Cloud, *Changes That Heal: The Four Shifts That Make Everything Better . . . and That Everyone Can Do* (Grand Rapids: Zondervan, 1992), 62.

3. Brené Brown, *Daring Greatly: How the Courage to Be Vulnerable Transforms the Way We Live, Love, Parent, and Lead* (New York: Gotham, 2012), 34.

4. Undesirability

1. C. S. Lewis, *The Complete C. S. Lewis Signature Classics*, rev. ed. (Grand Rapids: Zondervan, 2002), 406.

6. Exposure

1. Matthew Henry, *Matthew Henry's Concise Commentary on the Bible*, Christian Classics Ethereal Library, www.ccel.org/ccel/henry/mhcc.l.vi.html.

7. Jealousy

1. Andrea Lucado, "One Way to Keep Jealousy from Stealing Your Joy," *Storyline* (blog), http://storylineblog.com/2016/09/15one-way-to-keep-jealousy-from-stealing-your-joy/.

2. Lysa TerKeurst, "A Cure for Jealousy," LysaTerKeurst.com, July 13, 2011, http://lysaterkeurst.com/2011/07/a-cure-for-jealousy/.

3. Shauna Niequist, *Bittersweet: Thoughts on Change, Grace, and Learning the Hard Way* (Grand Rapids: Zondervan, 2013), 112.

8. Faithlessness

1. C. S. Lewis, *Mere Christianity* (New York: HarperCollins, 2001), 147–48.

2. *Webster's Collegiate Dictionary*, s.v. "worship," www.webstersdictionary1828.com/Dictionary/worship.

3. Sarah Bessey, "Joy: Third Sunday of Advent," December 24, 2015, http://sarahbessey.com/joy-third-sunday-of-advent/.

4. James Hastings, *The Great Texts of the Bible: Saint John XIII-XXI* (New York: Charles Scribner's Sons, 1912), 170.

9. Bitterness

1. Shauna Niequist, *Bittersweet: Thoughts on Change, Grace, and Learning the Hard Way* (Grand Rapids: Zondervan, 2013), 11.

2. Raechel Myers, "Jesus Is the True & Better Adam," She Reads Truth website, November 30, 2015, http://shereadstruth.com/2015/11/30/jesus-is-the-true-better-adam/.

3. Sara Hagerty, *Every Bitter Thing Is Sweet: Tasting the Goodness of God in All Things* (Grand Rapids: Zondervan, 2014), 185.

4. James Strong, *Strong's Exhaustive Concordance of the Bible* (Nashville: Abingdon Press, 1890), s.v. "paraklesis."

10. Hopelessness

1. Matthew Henry, *Matthew Henry's Concise Commentary on the Bible*, Christian Classics Ethereal Library, accessed August 22, 2017, www.ccel.org/ccel/henry/mhcc.l.vi.html.

2. "Hebrews 10:22-23 Commentary," February 24, 2015, Precept Austin, www.preceptaustin.org/hebrews_1022-23.

3. David Murray, "10 Reasons to Hope (When All Seems Hopeless)," Ligonier Ministries, February 4, 2013, www.ligonier.org/blog/10-reasons-hope-when-all-seems-hopeless/.

11. Loss

1. Paula Rinehart, *Strong Women, Soft Hearts* (Nashville: Thomas Nelson, 2001), 9–10.

2. Alexander MacLaren, *Expositions of Holy Scripture* (Grand Rapids: Baker Books, 1974), http://biblehub.com/commentaries/maclaren/isaiah/61.htm.

3. Mary Elizabeth Byrne, trans., "Be Thou My Vision," Hymnary.org, accessed August 22, 2017, http://hymnary.org/text/be_thou_my_vision_o_lord_of_my_heart.

12. Fear

1. Stasi Eldredge, Facebook post, January 14, 2017, www.facebook.com/StasiEldredge/posts/1066477010165139.

2. Donald Miller, *A Million Miles in a Thousand Years: How I Learned to Live a Better Story* (Nashville: Thomas Nelson, 2009), 108.

Looking for a way to dig deeper into the *never alone* message through Bible study?

Embrace your incredible value and indispensable role in the Kingdom today!

In the six-week Bible study, *Never Alone: 6 Encounters with Jesus to Heal Your Deepest Hurts*, Tiffany reveals the depth and healing power of Jesus' unconditional love for us through a refreshing look at encounters He had with six hurting women in the Gospels. Meet the woman caught in adultery, the hemorrhaging woman, the woman at the well, the woman who anointed Him, Mary Magdalene, and Mary the mother of Jesus whose life-changing interactions reveal a compassionate Redeemer who offers healing from your deepest hurts, hope, second chances, grace-giving love, and companionship.

Participant Workbook, Leader Guide, DVD, and Leader Kit available.

Participant Workbook | 9781501845826   Leader Guide | 978151845840
DVD | 9781501845864   Leader Kit | 9781501845871

Find Samples and Resources at AbingdonWomen.com/TiffanyBluhm

Available Wherever Books are Sold.

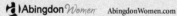 Abingdon *Women*   AbingdonWomen.com